AF846417

CYCLING THE CAMINO PORTUGUÉS

FROM LISBON AND PORTO TO SANTIAGO DE COMPOSTELA

by John Hayes

CICERONE

JUNIPER HOUSE, MURLEY MOSS,
OXENHOLME ROAD, KENDAL, CUMBRIA LA9 7RL
cicerone.co.uk

© John Hayes 2026
First edition 2026
ISBN: 978 1 78631 304 1
eISBN: 978 1 78765 273 6

MIX
Paper | Supporting responsible forestry
FSC® C014138

Printed in Czechia on responsibly sourced paper on behalf of Latitude Press Ltd.
A catalogue record for this book is available from the British Library.
All photographs are by the author unless otherwise stated.

lovelljohns.com

Route mapping by Lovell Johns lovelljohns.com
Contains OpenStreetMap.org data © OpenStreetMap contributors, CC-BY-SA.
NASA relief data courtesy of ESRI

Cicerone's EU representative for GPSR compliance is Easy Access System Europe, Mustamäe tee 50, 10621 Tallinn, Estonia. Email gpsr.requests@easproject.com.

Updates to this guide

While we strive to ensure that our guidebooks are as up to date and accurate as possible, changes can occur during the lifetime of an edition. Facilities, accommodation, transport and even rights of way can change, so if you find any inaccuracies in this book or have any feedback, please let us know by email at updates@cicerone.co.uk. Updates will be published on the Cicerone website (cicerone.co.uk/1304/updates), so please check before planning your trip.

To receive free updates, special offers and GPX files where available, don't forget to register your book at the 'My Account' tab at cicerone.co.uk.

Front cover: A tough hill in the forest approaching Tomar

CONTENTS

Acknowledgements

Many thanks to Robina, Mike, and Christine who cycled with me on my first Camino trip finding the bits you can now avoid. Particular thanks to Mike for many of the photos.

Not recommended! Stage 3 of the Coastal Camino north of Viano do Castelo

ROUTE SUMMARY TABLE

Stage	Start	Finish	Distance	Ascent	Descent	Time	Page
Lisbon to Porto on the Central Camino							
1	Lisbon	Vila Franca de Xira	40km	153m	153m	3hr	45
2	Vila Franca de Xira	Santarém	53km	121m	23m	4hr	51
3	Santerém	Tomar	64km	304m	363m	4hr 40min	56
4	Tomar	Ansião	47km	767m	608m	4hr 10min	63
5	Ansião	Coimbra	47km	530m	714m	4hr	67
6	Coimbra	Albergaria-a-Velha	65km	504m	403m	5hr	74
7	Albergaria-a-Velha	Porto	71.2km	782m	894m	5hr 40min	79
Porto to Santiago de Compostela							
The Central Camino							
1	Porto	Barcelos	64km	463m	412m	5hr 15min	94
2	Barcelos	Valença/Tui	73km	1012m	1008m	6hr 15min	99
3	Valença/Tui	Pontevedra	55.5km	654m	656m	4hr 50min	104
4	Pontevedra	Santiago de Compostela	64.5km	685m	438m	5hr 15min	110
The Coastal Camino							
1	Porto	Vila do Conde	29.4km	47m	47m	2hr 10min	118
2	Vila do Conde	Viana do Castelo	52km	270m	263m	4hr	122
3	Viana do Castelo	A Guarda	36.5km	150m	144m	2hr 40min	128
Link route	Caminha	Valença/Tui on the Central Camino	30.5km	350m	330m	2hr 10min	132
4	A Guarda	Vigo	58km	395m	333m	5hr	136
5	Vigo	Pontevedra	36.8km	476m	511m	4hr 15min	141
The Spiritual Variant							
1	Pontevedra	Padrón	78.2km	850m	850m	7hr	146

STAGE FACILITIES PLANNER

- Accommodation
- Refreshments
- Shop
- Bike shop
- Tourist information
- Train station

From Lisbon to Porto on the Central Camino

Stage	Location	Intermediate Distance	Time	Facilities					
1	**Lisbon**	**-**	**-**	Accommodation	Refreshments	Shop	Bike shop	Tourist information	Train station
1	**Vila Franca de Xira**	**40km**	**3hr**	Accommodation	Refreshments		Bike shop		Train station
2	Vila Nova da Rainha	11.3km	50min		Refreshments				
2	**Santarém**	**41.7km**	**3hr 10min**	Accommodation	Refreshments			Tourist information	Train station
3	**Tomar**	**64km**	**4hr 40min**	Accommodation	Refreshments		Bike shop		Train station
4	Alviobeira	11.2km	1hr		Refreshments				
4	Areias	9.2km	50min		Refreshments	Shop			
4	Alvaiázere	12km	1hr 5min	Accommodation	Refreshments	Shop			
4	**Ansião**	**14.6km**	**1hr 20min**	Accommodation	Refreshments	Shop			
5	Alvorge	10.2km	50min	Accommodation	Refreshments				
5	Rabaçal	8.1km	40min	Accommodation	Refreshments				
5	**Coimbra**	**28.7km**	**2hr 25min**	Accommodation	Refreshments				Train station
6	Mealhada	23.9km	1hr 50min		Refreshments		Bike shop		
6	Águeda	24.8km	1hr 55min	Accommodation	Refreshments		Bike shop		
6	**Albergaria-a-Velha**	**16.4km**	**1hr 15min**	Accommodation	Refreshments				
7	Pinheiro da Bemposta	12.4km	1hr		Refreshments				
7	Mafamude	50.3km	4hr	Accommodation					
7	**Porto**	**8.5km**	**40min**	Accommodation	Refreshments	Shop	Bike shop	Tourist information	Train station

From Porto to Santiago de Compostela on the Central Camino

Stage	Location	Intermediate Distance	Time	Facilities					
1	**Porto**	**-**	**-**	⌂	🍴	🧺	⚙	ℹ	■
1	Azurara	31km	2hr 35min	⌂					
1	Barcelinhos	32.4km	2hr 40min	⌂	🍴				
1	**Barcelos**	**0.6km**	**5min**	⌂	🍴		⚙		
2	Aborim	12km	1hr	⌂	🍴				
2	Seara	17km	1hr 25min				⚙		
2	Ponte de Lima	5km	25min	⌂	🍴		⚙	ℹ	
2	Rubiães	21.7km	1hr 50min		🍴				
2	Linhares	4.1km	20min		🍴				
2	**Valença/Tui**	**13.3km**	**1hr 10min**	⌂	🍴				■
3	O Porriño	18.7km	1hr 40min		🍴		⚙		
3	**Pontevedra**	**36.8km**	**3hr 10min**	⌂	🍴				■
4	Padrón	39.7km	3hr 15min	⌂					■
4	**Santiago de Compostela**	**24.8km**	**2hr**	⌂	🍴	🧺	⚙	ℹ	■

Narrow path, easily missed (Stage 5 of the Central Camino from Lisbon to Porto)

From Porto to Santiago de Compostela on the Coastal Camino

Stage	Location	Intermediate Distance	Time	Facilities
1	**Porto**	**-**	**-**	
1	Azurara	28.8km	2hr 5min	
1	**Vila do Conde**	**0.6km**	**5min**	
2	Bairro Piscatório	5.5km	25min	
2	Póvoa de Varzim	1.4km	5min	
2	**Viana do Castelo**	**45.1km**	**3hr 30min**	
3	*Lovelhe 11.1km off-route*			
3	Moledo	25km	1hr 50min	
3	Caminha	3.6km	15min	
3	**A Guarda**	**7.9km**	**35min**	
4	O Arrabal	13.2km	1hr 10min	
4	Percebelleira	13.2km	1hr 10min	
4	Baiona	4.8km	25min	
4	**Vigo**	**26.8km**	**2hr 20min**	
5	**Pontevedra**	**36.8km**	**4hr 15min**	

The Spiritual Variant

Stage	Location	Intermediate Distance	Time	Facilities
1	**Pontevedra**	**-**	**-**	
1	*Cambados 2.8 km off-route*			
1	O Convento	7.6km	40min	
1	A Escusa	12km	1hr 5min	
1	Mosteiro de Santa Maria da Armenteira	0.3km	5min	
1	Vilanova de Arousa	22.3km	2hr	
1	Vilagarcía de Arousa	12.4km	1hr 5min	
1	**Padrón**	**23.7km**	**2hr 5min**	

The ritual of leaving a stone is a symbolic act for many pilgrims (Stage 4 of the Coastal Camino)

The off-road stretch after Alvorge (Stage 5 of the Central Camino from Lisbon to Porto)

Journey's end

INTRODUCTION

The lovely bridge south of Arcos (Stage 1 of the Central Camino from Porto to Santiago de Compostela)

In terms of numbers, the Camino Portugués (Spanish spelling, and Caminho Português in Portuguese) is the second most popular route (after the French Way) for pilgrims travelling to Santiago de Compostela. The route connects three of the world's most beautiful cities: Lisbon, Porto and Santiago de Compostela and, give or take a few years, is as old as Portugal itself. In the 11th and 12th centuries, pilgrims were already heading north as the Christian invasion moved south with the parents of Portugal's first king (Alfonso I), Count Henrique and Dona Teresa, making the journey in 1097.

Experienced pilgrims will have their own favourite, but many argue that the Camino Portugués is the most beautiful of all the pilgrim routes to Santiago de Compostela. Following empty country roads and farm tracks, the route from Lisbon to Porto is quiet, and the small number of pilgrims disappears into a landscape that shifts from flat farmland to forest and hills. From Porto to Santiago de Compostela, things get busier with the larger numbers of pilgrims catered for by an additional Coastal Camino. The Coastal Camino visits important historic shipbuilding and fishing ports central to Portugal's rich maritime

Ponte Sampaio north of Redondela (Stage 3 of the Central Camino from Porto to Santiago de Compostela)

history, before crossing into Spain to experience the classic Galician coastline. The Central Camino follows a more direct, mountainous route, crossing into Spain at Valença.

Lisbon, Porto, and Santiago de Compostela feature on many travellers' bucket lists of must-see cities. With nearby international airports, Portugal's two biggest cities are particularly busy, but there are plenty of other attractions on the Camino. These include, on the Lisbon–Porto leg, Santerém, Tomar and Coimbra, which feature UNESCO World Heritage sites, and on the Porto–Santiago de Compostela leg, the stunning town of Viana do Castelo or the border towns of Valença/Tui.

Irrespective of personal religion, the experience of travelling along a Camino is unique. The journey, shared with travellers from around the world, alone or in groups, often celebrating a lifetime milestone, is intensely communal. The journey means that everyone has something in common, and despite language barriers, conversation is easy.

The Camino Portugués is not a journey for travellers seeking solitude. To qualify as a pilgrim, walkers need to complete 100km and cyclists 200km. These distances matter, and most pilgrims start a 243km journey to Santiago de Compostela in Porto rather than from Lisbon, which is 621km away.

Cycling the Camino is, of course, different to walking it. Travelling so much faster means you're unlikely to meet a walker more than once. Cyclists, however, are recognised by walkers as fellow pilgrims who exchange the same friendly greetings. With a growing number of adventure travel companies offering the Camino as a cycling holiday, the number of cyclists has increased, but it remains small relative to walkers.

The Camino is very well waymarked. It is, however, not a curated cycling route (such as a EuroVelo). The yellow arrows, used to direct walking pilgrims, don't always work for cyclists. To avoid travelling the wrong way up one-way streets, some frankly dangerous stretches of urban cycling (particularly in Lisbon and Porto), and the occasional need to carry bikes up and over rugged terrain, the route needs to be tweaked to make it bike-friendly.

While the Camino is a significant feature of the Portuguese and Spanish tourism industries and promoted by both governments, the route has a degree of informality. The waymarking is excellent, but it does change, and maps, digital or otherwise, struggle to keep up. Pilgrims are often more interested in the destination than in the route, and the route changes as better alternatives develop through practice.

THE ROUTE TO SANTIAGO DE COMPOSTELA

Legend has it that James, a cousin of Jesus and brother of John, and, along with Peter, one of the first three apostles, returned to Jerusalem after preaching in Iberia and was the first apostle martyred in AD44. His body (not his head) returned to Galicia on a rudderless stone boat guided by angels and was buried in a tomb on Mount Libredón. In the early ninth century, a hermit named Pelayo discovered the tomb (using the stars shining on a field), and informed the local bishop, who relayed the news to King Alfonso II of Asturias, who then ordered the construction of the first of a series of churches on the site.

At the time, Muslims controlled most of the Iberian Peninsula and also occupied other potential pilgrimage destinations around Jerusalem. The only way for pilgrims from the rest of Europe to get to Santiago de Compostela was through a narrow strip of land still controlled by Christians to the north of the Cantabrian mountains. New pilgrimage opportunities opened up in the 12th century with the Reconquest and the founding of the Kingdom of Portugal; as Christians moved south, the new Camino Portugués route lengthened.

The Central Camino

The Central Camino, from Lisbon to Santiago de Compostela, is 621km long or 243km from Porto. The route has changed in detail over time, but an itinerary, often utilising Roman roads, was established by the Middle Ages.

Cycling from Lisbon to Porto along the Central Camino, without

Approaching Porto Santa María de Oia (Stage 4 of the Coastal Camino)

any stopovers, can be comfortably completed in seven days. The route visits the historic towns/cities of Santerém, Tomar and Coimbra. You reach Santerém after two days of relatively easy cycling across a flat agricultural landscape, with the route becoming more challenging on the approach to Tomar on Day 3. The following two days, through to Coimbra, involve some remote and hilly cycling, including a 480m pass. For the last two days, on the run-in to Porto, the days are slightly longer, but the cycling, a mix of rural and suburban, is easy.

It is possible to complete the journey from Porto to Santiago de Compostela in four days, with stops at Braga, Barcelos, Valença/Tui, and Pontevedra. However, the third day, depending on the itinerary, may be challenging. Combining the two legs of the Central Camino means that the whole route, without stopovers, could be completed in 11 days.

The Coastal Camino and the Sendero Litoral

Although the Coastal Camino has a multi-century pedigree, is waymarked, and is defined on the map base, the route in practice is more dynamic. Nominally, the route heads up the coast from Porto, visiting Vila do Conde and Viana do Castelo. One version has it crossing the River Minho and the border by ferry at Caminha, then continuing along the coast to

Vigo to join the Central Camino at Redondela, while the other stays on the south bank of the river and joins the Central Camino at Valença.

The problem with the Coastal Camino is that it's not always that coastal. Pilgrims have voted with their feet and, whenever possible, follow footpaths closer to the coastline, including the Sendero Litoral, which is also waymarked with yellow arrows.

The Spiritual Variant

Rather than taking the direct route from Pontevedra to Padrón (39km), the Spiritual way heads west along the southern coast of a peninsula, climbs over it and then heads east along its northern coast to Padrón (78km). Although the Spiritual Variant features the route's most challenging climb, it requires only a single day of cycling. If 78km and a climb are too much, there are plenty of places to stay on the route, or you could reduce the journey to 46km by catching a ferry. The Traslatio Route makes the same journey as the boat carrying St James' body in AD44.

THE CYCLING

The Camino is designed for walking pilgrims and presents occasional challenges that most cyclists will want to avoid. The guide and associated app identify a recommended route that excludes segments of the Camino where cycling is illegal (one-way streets or walkways where cycling is not allowed), avoids dangerous sections in Lisbon and Porto, and avoids segments that require carrying a bike or are otherwise difficult. The actual Camino is included as an alternative route in the bike-carrying or difficult cycling category, for cyclists who relish a challenge.

The research for the guide involved the author in two journeys. The first, with three other cyclists, followed the Camino almost in its entirety (although some of it in the wrong direction), finding, in an occasionally painful way, the unpleasant bits. The journey included the Coastal, Central and Spiritual variants. The

Hard going north of Viana do Castelo (Stage 3, Coastal Camino)

second, a solo journey, tested alternatives, filled in gaps, and, because the weather was bad, discovered how rain affected the route.

For most of the time, the recommended route follows the Camino on quiet country roads with very little traffic. There are off-road sections, usually along agricultural or forest tracks used by vehicles, with the route occasionally being a single track. The waymarking on the Camino is generally excellent and, apart from the recommended variations, is easy to follow without GPS, a map, or a guide.

The Camino passes through the heart of the ancient, hilly cities of Lisbon and Porto. For the first-time visitor, these cities are not pleasant places to cycle – even dangerous. Rather than following the Camino, the recommended route provides safer ways out of cities.

One challenge, unfortunately, can't be mitigated: the *calçada portuguesa*. This is a pavement surface material, similar to cobblestones but technically composed of limestone sets, found throughout the country and worldwide in places with a Portuguese connection. Regarding the route, the surface is more common on roads in built-up areas, particularly in cycling routes around Porto. It's an uncomfortable cycling surface and ends abruptly once you get to Spain.

The Camino Portugués, if the recommended route is adopted, is an excellent route for touring cyclists. It is, however, a mixed surface and doesn't work for road cyclists. See below for recommendations on choosing a bike.

GEOGRAPHY AND HISTORY

Cycling the Camino is a fundamentally different experience to walking it – and inevitably, a two-week trip is less immersive than a two-month one. There is a lot to see, geographically, historically and culturally, and making sense of it all at pace is a challenge. Accepting that a bit of knowledge is a dangerous thing, this section highlights a few features that might help.

The geography

It might be stating the obvious, but the location of Portugal and Galicia on the western side of the Iberian Peninsula is significant. Although the route runs from south to north, the physical geography runs from east to west. In particular, five rivers flow westward from the *mesata* (the plateau covering much of the Iberian peninsula) into the Atlantic. The longest, the Tagus, rises in eastern Spain, 150km from the Mediterranean, before emerging into the ocean after 1007km at Lisbon. Perhaps the most beautiful is the Douro (the Douro Valley is a UNESCO World Heritage Site), which contributes to Porto's spectacular location. The east–west-running rivers, their bridges, ferries, and valleys provide an underpinning structure for the journey.

The climate is Mediterranean (hot and dry in summer and wet in winter), but Atlantic influence increases the probability of precipitation toward the north.

Forests and woodlands (36% of land use in Portugal) feature prominently along the route in both Portugal and Galicia, with trees typical of the Mediterranean, including various evergreen oak species, maritime pine, cedar and ash. There is also extensive eucalyptus (introduced for the paper industry), and the crunchy tree litter along the route through these forests makes for an interesting cycling surface.

The history

One of the joys of cycling from place to place is trying to unpick the story behind the towns and buildings – the things that resonate with places you're familiar with and the things that are surprising and different.

Pre-Roman

Many of the towns had already been settled, on a small scale, before the Romans arrived in the third centuryBC. In southern Portugal, Lisbon was founded by the Phoenicians, whereas Porto, in central Portugal, was founded by the Lusitanians, a Celtic tribe. Galicia takes its name from the Gallaeci, another Celtic tribe, who were associated with 'Castro culture', the fortified hilltop villages known as *castros*. There are such villages at A Guarda and Vigo.

Mosaic at Conimbriga (Stage 5 of the Central Camino from Lisbon to Porto)

The Romans

The Romans expanded the administrative centres (particularly Lisbon, Santarém, and Coimbra) and constructed the connections between them, many of which remain in use today. Roman roads (*via Romana*) feature on various sections of the Camino, in particular the Via XIX and the Via XVI and the river crossings frequently employ medieval bridges built on Roman foundations. Spanish, Portuguese and Galician are all Latin languages, inherited from the six or seven centuries of Roman domination. During this period, they also introduced wine and olive oil production, crops that remain prominent in agriculture today, and fish salting. Salted fish is a core component of the Portuguese and Spanish diets.

The central octagon in Tomar's Convent of Christ (Stage 3 of the Central Camino from Lisbon to Porto)

The Visigoths

The Visigoths arrived in the Iberian Peninsula, having been driven out of France by the Franks, as the Roman Empire fell in the fourth century. More than the invaders/migrants in post-Roman Britain, the Visigoths absorbed the Roman legacy, abandoned their native language, developed a Latin-based vernacular, converted to Christianity (initially in their own rite), and built churches in the Roman style. The Visigothic Iberian Kingdom fell to the Muslim invasion of 711, a date generally used to mark the end of the Visigothic period. Arguably, the Visigothic kingdom persisted north of the Cantabrian Mountains and served as the basis for the Kingdom of Asturias, which was crucial to the origins of the St James Way.

The Muslims

Muslims were in Portugal for five centuries, until 1249, although the periods of Muslim domination and Reconquest overlapped, and their impact was less significant north of the Douro. Today, the Muslim legacy is evident in place names (Alfama and Benfica in Lisbon); vocabulary (*azeitona* (olive), *alface* (lettuce), *arroz* (rice); decorative arts, in particular the iconic *azulejos* (ceramic tiles); and in some buildings (mainly in the Algarve). The architectural style inherited from the Muslims (the Mudéjar) – horseshoe arches, geometric brickwork, and intricate tiles – persisted long after the Muslim power, sometimes worked on by the Muslim artisans who remained in the country.

The Reconquest

Portugal, as a separate country, emerged from the process of 'reconquest'. The border between the Muslim and Christian worlds was fluid from the 8th to the 12th centuries (around the Doura), and in the north-west, there were separate kingdoms of Galicia, Asturias, and León, and a county of Portugal (not ruled by a King). In the early 12th century, following a dispute between the King of León (Alphonso VII) and his cousin Alphonso of Portugal, a treaty was brokered by the Catholic bishop of Braga at Zamora (1143) that resulted in the county of Portugal becoming a separate kingdom.

Although Muslims maintained a presence in Iberia until the late 15th century, the bulk of the Reconquest occurred in the 12th and 13th centuries, when it became an Iberian wing of the Crusades. Crusaders from the north (Normans, English, Norwegians) on the way to the Holy Lands rested at Porto and joined in the Reconquest. For example, the final conquest of Lisbon combined a force of 3000 Portuguese marching down from Coimbra with 13,000 crusaders who sailed up the Tagus.

The Reconquest legacy produced a distinct Romanesque architectural style in the cathedrals of Lisbon, Tomar, Coimbra and Tui, buildings that combined religious and defensive functions. The characteristic rounded arches, typical of cathedrals across Europe in the period, are combined with the massive granite wall and narrow slits for windows typical of a castle.

The Age of Discovery and the Golden Age

Some historians argue that the Reconquest provided the momentum for a fantastic period of Portuguese global expansion. Aided by technical and navigational breakthroughs, in part sponsored by Henry the Navigator, Portugal established a sea-based global trading empire. Key milestones were: 1488, when Bartolomeu Dias rounded the Cape of Good Hope; 1498, when Vasco da Gama reached India, establishing a direct sea route to the East; and 1500, when Pedro Álvares Cabral 'accidentally' discovered Brazil.

The revenues generated by the lucrative spice trade with India, in particular, and by the slave trade into its Brazilian possessions were extraordinary. Portugal quickly became one of the wealthiest countries in Europe and buildings constructed in the 15th and 16th centuries reflect this.

The Manueline Style (late 15th to early 16th century) – also known as Portuguese Late Gothic – is the architectural style associated with the Age of Discovery under King Manuel I, featuring flamboyant ornamentation often including maritime symbols such as ropes and anchors. In Spain, the Plateresque style, based on silver filigree, evolved at the same time. Incidentally, the cobbled road surface, the *calçada portuguesa*, was first used in Lisbon during the reign of King Manuel I.

Colonialism and protracted decline

The Golden Age came to a crashing end in 1578 at the disastrous Battle of Alcácer Quibir, when the Portuguese King (Sebastian) and much of the nobility were killed. The Battle resulted in the country's 60-year absorption into the Iberian Union with Spain in 1580. After its Golden Age, Portugal entered a protracted period of decline and the progressive loss of its overseas empire was a source of instability. A political football, Portugal suffered in the rivalry between England and Spain in the 17th century; between Britain and France in the Seven Years' War; and between Britain and France in the Peninsula War. Its involvement in the First World War was domestically disastrous despite fighting on the victorious side; the resulting turmoil enabled Salazar's dictatorship to endure from 1926 to 1974.

Portugal still held overseas colonies, particularly in Africa, and in the 1960s fought costly colonial wars in Angola, Mozambique, and Guinea-Bissau. The conflicts continued until 1974 and resulted in an estimated loss of life of 120,000 Africans, finally ending with a coup d'état in Portugal known as the Carnation Revolution. After a period of intense political instability, a democratically elected government was established (the Third Republic). The end of the colonial wars saw a million refugees admitted into Portugal, which at the time had a population of eight million.

In 1986, Portugal, along with Spain, joined the EU (then the EEC) and in 2002 introduced the Euro. Although the country suffered particularly badly following the 2007 financial crisis, it has experienced sustained progress in economic and welfare indicators, although on most measures it remains below the EU average.

Portugal's history, combined with its geography, was particularly dramatically illustrated in 1755 by the Lisbon earthquake. This extreme seismological event, and its subsequent tsunami, destroyed the city and killed an estimated 40,000 people.

CHOOSING YOUR ROUTE

Given the options north of Porto, there are lots of different ways to cycle to Santiago de Compostela.

To qualify as a pilgrim, you must walk 100km or cycle 200km. On the Camino Portugués, the number of walking pilgrims increases dramatically after Porto, with most pilgrims choosing Porto or Tui as their starting point and taking about two weeks to complete the journey. The shorter Central Camino is the most popular (63% of pilgrims), but the Coastal Camino is also busy, compared to the route from Lisbon to Porto.

Just north of Padrón (Stage 4 of the Central Camino from Porto to Santiago de Compostela)

Cyclists, travelling faster, have more options. If two weeks is the window, then you can do the entire route, from Lisbon to Santiago de Compostela, on either the Central or Coastal Camino in the available time.

There are no bad options between Porto and Santiago de Compostela, but choosing is a planning challenge. In addition to either the Central or Coastal Camino (both share the same final Stage to Santiago de Compostela), there are various combinations of routes as you cross from one to the other at Barcelos, Valença/Tui, and Redondela. In addition, you can add a day or two by cycling the Spiritual Variant.

Before making a decision, read the route descriptions in the rest of the guide and consider the different attractions of the stopovers.

Starting in Porto is another option worth considering – heading north on one Camino and returning to Porto on the other, something which again can be completed in two weeks. The advantage is that you can see all the sites north of Porto and fly in and out of the same airport, which is particularly advantageous if bringing your bike in a rigid bike box. It does mean travelling against the pilgrim traffic on one leg, but I did this with some friends when researching the book, and it wasn't a problem.

Ready to be packed

Finally, if time isn't an issue, starting and finishing in Lisbon is also an option. Head up to Santiago de Compostela on the Central Camino, return to Porto on the Coastal Camino and then follow the EuroVelo 1 south along the coast on a generally easy route, visiting the world's most famous surfing beaches en route.

PLANNING YOUR TRIP

When to go

The main pilgrimage 'season' is April to October, with July and August the busiest and hottest months. Compared with the rest of the Iberian Peninsula, the climate north of Lisbon is relatively mild; the main constraints being winter precipitation and limited accommodation.

Own bike or hire?

My bike fits me perfectly, has been on many journeys with me, and is like an old friend. Generally speaking, I take it everywhere and now know how to protect it from rough treatment by baggage handlers. Travelling with a bike, however, is a challenge, particularly for touring cyclists who start and finish at different destinations. Hiring a bike is now a proven alternative, with bike-hire companies in Lisbon and Porto that provide a service that includes collecting the bike from a hotel at the end of the route. Bike hire is the only option for cyclists who want to travel on an e-bike, as these bikes aren't allowed on passenger planes. The Appendix lists potential bike-hire companies.

Type of bike

The gravel bike category has broadened the choices available to touring cyclists, and I used a gravel bike with large tyres on both my trips. With the rough surfaces, particularly the *calçada portuguesa*, most cyclists will appreciate additional shock absorption, and all bike hire companies recommend a hardtail mountain bike for the route. An e-mountain bike is also a viable option if hired locally.

Getting there and back

If you're not taking your own bike, getting there and back is straightforward with plane and train options for Lisbon, Porto, and Santiago de Compostela. Bike hire companies generally deliver to a starting hotel and pick up the bike where you finish. One of the listed companies is located next to the starting point in Lisbon, so you can ensure the bike fits before setting off.

Things are more complicated, although substantially cheaper, if you take your own bike and fly. The standard rigid, bulky bike box is infeasible because the trip start and end points are different. In my previous cycling guidebook on the Ruta Vía de la Plata, I described an approach based on a large plastic bag; for more comprehensive advice, consult *Guide to taking your bike on an aeroplane* by Dan Joyce, freely available from Cycling UK. It's an excellent description of the options and explains how to pack your bike in either a bag or a box. The only thing I would add is that, with the Camino, there are bike shops in Santiago de Compostela that will pack your bike for the return trip, and the Spanish post office (*Correos*) provides a full return service. Some couriers will organise bike transport, but my personal experience with this option has been poor (due to Brexit-related complications), and for the time-critical outward trip, I would recommend travelling on the same flight. My only other tip is that very robust, light, flexible fabric bags are available on AliExpress at a reasonable price.

Accommodation

In addition to the usual accommodation criteria (price, amenities, location), arrangements for bike storage and access, including traffic, need to be considered. Most places have secure storage or let you keep your bike in your room, but it's worth checking, particularly if you're on an e-bike. Booking.com and Google Maps are both helpful in choosing accommodation and for the final step of determining the exact location.

Most of the recommended stopovers offer a choice of accommodation, and booking a day or two in advance is fine unless you're in a group or in the peak season or want to stay in a particular hotel. When booking, message

Monastery de Santa Clara – now a 5 star hotel (Stage 1, Coastal Camino)

the property and let them know you need a secure place for your bike.

Generally speaking, all the stopovers recommended in this guide offer accommodation options to suit a range of budgets and preferences. The guide identifies examples of cheap, mid-range and luxury choices selected because they are close to the route, but for a more comprehensive list, and recent reviews, refer to Google Maps and Booking.com.

The cheapest options are pilgrim *albergues* or hostels.

Pilgrim hostels are the traditional option for pilgrims and provide shared, often mixed, dormitory-style accommodation on a first-come, first-served basis. Frequently run by a pilgrim organisation, church, or municipality, accommodation is available only to pilgrims holding a pilgrim credential. They include facilities for washing clothes and preparing meals. Some still operate on a donation basis, but expect to pay between 10 and 20 Euros otherwise. If you're planning to use the pilgrim hostels, pack a lightweight sleeping bag.

Hostels are the budget option and are particularly suited to walking pilgrims doing the whole route. Reviews are mixed and often report noise, long queues to enter, and even bedbugs. They are, however, a distinct feature of the Camino experience and they are not all the same. Not all pilgrims stay in hostels, particularly those on shorter itineraries, who, frequently using 'bag ahead' services, are often to be found in hotels.

Not exclusive to pilgrims, private *albergues*, hostels and Youth Hostels often offer good value and usually include private rooms. Bookable in advance, Youth Hostels (Pousadas de Juventude) provide places for people of any age or nationality. Again, expect to pay between 10 and 20 Euros per person.

Mid-range accommodation in small hotels, bed-and-breakfasts, or room-only options is plentiful in Portugal and Spain and offers good value (particularly when compared to the UK). All types are available on Booking.com, although direct booking is sometimes cheaper, and contact details are available on Google Maps. Expect to pay between 40 and 80 Euros for a twin room.

For those less restricted by budget and willing to spend between 80 and 120 Euros on a twin room, you can stay in a castle. Most of the larger stopovers have *pousadas* (Portugal) or *paradores* (Spain), which are accommodation options established to make economic use of historic buildings. The parador in Santiago de Compostela, in the plaza next to the Cathedral, is wonderful, and perhaps the oldest hotel in the world. Paradors and pousadas can feel a little old-fashioned, and the food is good but not adventurous. They are, however, very reliable and the service is great and definitely a good option if within budget.

Food

Portugal and Spain continue to offer choice and excellent value in food and drink. In particular, there are still places for breakfast, a mid-morning coffee and pastry break, and lunch in towns and villages, where comparable venues in northern Europe no longer exist.

In Portugal, bakery/pastry shops are often community venues where locals gather for coffee, pastries (including the famous Pastel de Nata), and to play the lottery. Lunch is also a communal, local workers' preference, with a cheap sit-down meal preferred to takeaway. The menu of the day, usually three courses, is excellent value, and in some places a special pilgrims' menu is also provided.

The cuisine has a significant seafood component, including the ubiquitous salt cod (there are as many *bacalhau* recipes as days in the year), hearty meat stews (*cozido à portuguesa*), and the famous soup starter (*caldo verde*). Ingredients also reflect Portugal's colonial heritage, including sweet potatoes from Brazil and piri-piri peppers from Angola and Mozambique.

One dish unique to Portugal and ubiquitous around Porto is the *francesinha* ('little French girl'), based on the croque monsieur, made with toasted, sliced white bread, cheese and meat, and served in a rich gravy. For some reason, it has not gained the same international reputation as piri-piri chicken.

Padrón peppers

A significant difference between Portugal and Spain (Galicia) lies in mealtimes. Spain is on Central European Time, and mealtimes are much later than in Portugal (where mealtimes are similar to those in the UK). From a cycling perspective, this works well, as you can eat a late lunch after finishing cycling and checking into accommodation.

Galicia is Spain's most significant seafood and dairy region, has its own distinct cuisine, and enjoys an international fine-dining reputation. Classic dishes include boiled octopus (*pulpo a la gallega*), hearty soups such as *caldo gallego*, Padrón peppers (*pimentos de Padrón*), and, of course, *tarta de Santiago*, which is ubiquitous in Santiago de Compostela. *Percebes* (goose neck barnacle) is an exceptional Galician seafood and, taken along with tarta de Santiago and a glass of Galician white wine (Albariño or Godello), could form the basis for a treat on arrival in Santiago de Compostela.

The Spanish and Portuguese eat a lot of meat (particularly pork), and the choice is more limited if you're a vegetarian. If the host seems friendly, and they usually are, a strategy I use is to let them know about my dietary preference and see what suggestions they come up with – the options suggested are often better than those presented on the menu.

Where lunch and coffee stops are few and far between, the app identifies potential venues; otherwise, the sheer volume of choice makes such information of little value. From Porto onward, the selection of restaurants and hotels improves, and there are notable venues that cyclists with a particular interest in food and distinctive places to stay might want to build a schedule around. These are described in the app.

Markets and market days

Municipal markets are thriving in both Spain and Portugal, and, as well as being interesting places to visit, they are often a go-to for in-situ food consumption. Communal eating is something the Spanish, in particular, enjoy, so consider heading to the market in all the larger destinations (Lisbon, Coimbra, Porto, Vigo, Santiago de Compostela).

All things being equal, arriving or leaving a town on market day adds to the fun, and sometimes this is another opportunity for communal eating (particularly in Padrón). Some markets are really special, Barcelos in particular, and in the summer, they attract visitors from far away.

Festivals

Festivals are an essential feature of life in Spain and Portugal, occurring in all but the smallest villages and often lasting multiple days. The excuses for having a festival are wide-ranging and include religious themes, the celebration of a renowned local product (usually a type of food), or a distinctive activity. June is peak festival time in Portugal, when many saints' days are celebrated. Festivals can be embraced or avoided; the latter is often advisable because some are so popular that securing accommodation can be difficult. Some of the key festivals are presented in the Appendix.

Alongside festivals, Camino Jubilee years are also a consideration in planning. When the Feast of St James the Apostle (July 25th) falls on a Sunday, it's a Jubilee Year. In a Jubilee year, the Holy Door (*Porta Santa*) in Santiago de Compostela Cathedral opens, allowing pilgrims to obtain plenary indulgences (the forgiveness of sins), and the Camino is even busier than usual.

What to take

Bike-packing mountain bikers have transformed the approach to cycle touring luggage with oversized saddle bags and front handlebar bags replacing the more traditional panniers. Panniers can carry more and are easier to detach from the bike, but for style, this approach has much going for it. Either way, the aim should be to avoid unnecessary weight.

For cycling gear, taking two of everything that has direct skin contact is a good rule of thumb. While it should be possible to wash and

Traveling light (Stage 1, Coastal Camino)

dry an outfit every night, a backup is advisable, given the small extra weight. There is a reasonable chance of some rain as you head north, so take a waterproof top. Additionally, a midweight fleece or merino cardigan suitable for evening wear makes sense. Helmets are a legal requirement in Spain and the right choice in Portugal, given those cobbles. Cycling shoes (MTB style), a cap and gloves are recommended, but a matter of preference.

Pack a pair of lightweight hiking trousers and a couple of T-shirts plus a pair of lightweight trainers for time off the bike. Toiletries should include a first-aid kit, travel wash and suntan lotion.

Essential for most travellers is a phone (potentially mounted on the bike for navigation), and, if the phone's camera is deemed inadequate, a camera, along with all chargers and adapters.

For the bike, you should have a bell, a pump, and drink containers. Although you're unlikely to be cycling in the dark, lights are essential in bad weather. Carry a multi-tool with a chain-repair tool and a spare link (it is unlikely that you will need it). If your bike has a derailleur hanger (the connector between the frame and the derailleur), take a spare one. Take spare inner tubes and a puncture repair kit. Depending on the distance, take some bike lubricant and a rag to remove excess oil.

If there isn't a secure bike store (often the luggage store), I keep my bike in my bedroom, which means I rarely need to lock it. I do, however, carry a lightweight lock. If new to cycle touring, complete a bike maintenance course before your journey. With luck, none of the skills acquired will be needed (touring tyres are highly puncture-resistant), but a course would build confidence.

The route is well served by cycle shops, and bike mechanics are part of a warm, international fraternity of cycling enthusiasts who will readily help a traveller.

USING THIS GUIDE

Cicerone app and GPX files

The primary purpose of this guide is to help cyclists decide whether this is the adventure for them; to help them plan and prepare for their adventure; to describe each day's cycling, what to watch out for, and where there are options; and to provide the information needed to make a choice.

GPX files are also available for download from cicerone.co.uk/1304 to be used in your own GPS or mapping apps. If you're not familiar with using a GPS app in a hiking or cycling context, it is a good idea to familiarise yourself with it before embarking on your trip. Lisbon on your first day is not an ideal training ground.

The Camino is well waymarked and, in general, a combination of yellow arrows and ordinary road signs makes navigation easy. There are navigation challenges along the route though, and the recommended route sometimes diverges from the Camino; consult the guide before starting each day, but otherwise keep it in reserve.

Navigation outside the towns is usually straightforward: signs are easier to spot, and navigation choices are limited. Most of the challenges occur in towns and cities where one-way systems are prevalent. The recommended route resolves many of these issues, but it won't direct you to your chosen hotel or hostel. To avoid a frustrating end to the day's cycling, use Google Maps to locate the accommodation and plan the final approach.

The guide can also be read in conjunction with the app, which provides GPS-enabled maps you can download for offline navigation, alternatives to the recommended route, location of key facilities and points of interest. You can buy the app version directly in the Cicerone app. The Cicerone app on a smartphone attached to the bike is the best way to navigate when the route diverges from the Camino. A smartphone can be connected to the bike using a mount, such as a Quad Lock mount, so you can follow the route as you cycle.

Add a stone and make a wish (Stage 4, Coastal Camino)

PILGRIM STAMPS

Full disclosure, I didn't collect pilgrim stamps on any of my Camino trips (I've now done four). Still, a pilgrim passport (*credencial*) is required to access pilgrim hostels and to obtain the official certificate of completion (*Compostela*). It is, of course, a personal memento and qualifies holders for various discounts at museums and some shops. A passport is available at key starting points, particularly the cathedrals in Lisbon, Porto, and Tui, and hotel and café owners will offer to stamp it as you progress along the route. It needs at least two stamps a day for the last 100km. Once the minimum requirements have been met (200km of cycling), pilgrims can collect the Compostela at the Pilgrim's Office in Santiago.

Acknowledging my grinch-like tendencies, I didn't attach a scallop shell, the universal pilgrim symbol, to my bike, which possibly explains the abysmal weather I experienced on my final Camino Portugués trip. I will not make the same mistake again.

Painted ceiling of the cathedral at Santarém (Stage 2 of the Central Camino from Lisbon to Porto)

Sub-Ripas Palace Coimbra

LISBON TO PORTO ON THE CENTRAL CAMINO

Porto
7 Albergaria-a-Velha
6 Coimbra
5 Ansião
4 Tomar
3 Santarém
2 Vila Franca de Xira
1
Lisbon

INTRODUCTION

Wildflowers on the bank of the Rio Trancão (Stage 1 of the Central Camino from Lisbon to Porto)

The Central Camino, from Lisbon to Porto, is 387km long, involves 3161m of elevation gain, and can be comfortably completed in seven days. Starting on Day 1 in Lisbon, the recommended schedule includes stops at Vila Franca de Xira, Santarém, Tomar, Ansião, Coimbra, and Albergaria-a-Velha, concluding in Porto on Day 7. There is a lot to see in Santarém, Tomar, and Coimbra; not so much in Ansião and Albergaria-a-Velha.

The route heads north along the western edge of the *mesata*, the central plateau of the Iberian Peninsula, and the eastern edge of the coastal plain, and is never more than 40km from the sea. In broad terms, there are three phases to the cycling: a flat first three days when it heads into the Ribatejo defined by the fertile plains of the Tagus River; two days through the central highlands, relatively empty and undulating with the route connecting a series of small towns; and a final two days, on the approach to Porto, where the route is easy but busier, still rural but with occasional industrial warehousing.

None of the days exceeds five hours on the bike, and the first just three. If the weather is bad or you want more time to visit Tomar and Coimbra, there are shortcut options.

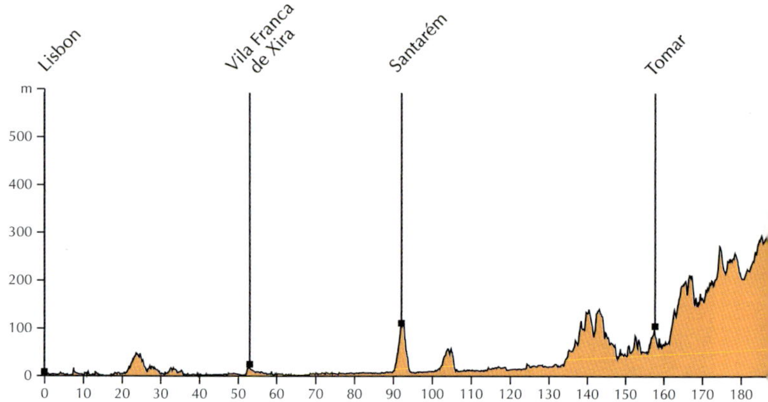

If you haven't been to Porto, it's definitely worth an extra day, and, if you want a break on the way, Coimbra is the obvious candidate.

For a faster journey, consider cycling to Santerém on Day 1. It's 93km, but aside from a climb at the end, it's easy cycling.

ARRIVING IN LISBON

Most international travellers arrive in Lisbon at the airport, located on the northern side of the city, 7km from the centre and the Day 1 starting point. Navigating an unfamiliar city by bike can lead to accidents, so choose accommodation that is easy to find and reasonably close to the route.

The simplest way to the city centre follows the main road south, which is straight and gently descending. Central Lisbon is busy with lots of one-way streets – on arrival, consider stopping, having a coffee in one of its lovely on-street cafés, and finding out where you are before planning your route to your hotel. Hopefully it's just a few metres away.

The airport is close to the Parque das Nações (3.6km) and the Camino. To avoid cycling into central Lisbon, staying near the Parque das Nações, which has many attractions in its own right, makes sense. Getting into Central Lisbon on public transport from the Parque das Nações is easy, and leaving on the Camino couldn't be more straightforward.

ARRIVING IN PORTO

Central Porto is a difficult place for a first-time visiting cyclist. It's hilly, with many cobbled one-way streets, and cycling there is hazardous. To

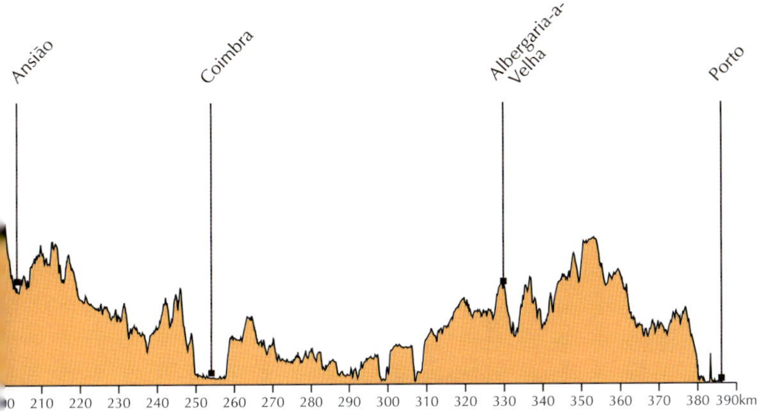

minimise city cycling, the recommended route crosses the iconic Luís I Bridge via its lower deck and heads west along the north bank of the River Douro. When leaving Porto, the recommended route, for both the Central and Coastal Caminos, heads up the coast to Vila do Conde. There is plenty of accommodation in Porto close to the recommended route, including accommodation on the south bank.

The view of the Ribeira district from the Dom Luís I Bridge (Stage 7 of the Central Camino from Lisbon to Porto)

Lisbon tram

Santa Justa Lift in Lisbon

Lisbon Cathedral

LISBON

Lisbon is the second-oldest city in Western Europe (beaten only by Athens) and has attracted successive waves of inhabitants since the Phoenicians first arrived around 1200BC. Its key strength is its sheltered harbour location. The city flourished, particularly as a global trade hub and the capital of Portugal's vast empire during the 15th- and 16th-century Age of Discovery, accumulating immense wealth. It suffered a catastrophic earthquake and tsunami in 1755 and, led by the Marquis of Pombal, was rebuilt with a modern grid pattern.

Lisbon, the capital of Portugal, has a population of approximately

FADO

The Central Camino starts in Lisbon and visits Coimbra, the two centres of *fado*, a traditional and much-venerated Portuguese singing genre. Fado is all about emotion (fado means 'fate') – usually expressing longing and nostalgia for something that has gone. Originating in 19th-century taverns, the solo singer (*fadista*), usually accompanied by a classical guitar, attempts to pull the audience into an intimate shared experience. Fado is intensely emotional in both cities; in Coimbra, it is associated with the university and sung by male students wearing the traditional student attire (*capa e betina*). Fado venues are easy to find in both cities.

600,000 and over three million in the wider metropolitan area.

With its international airport, low-cost flights from northern Europe, and favourable weather, Lisbon attracts large numbers of visitors. There is a lot to see.

The oldest neighbourhood and the best place to stroll and photograph the classic yellow trams is Alfama. The Alfama defined the city's boundaries until the Reconquest in 1147 and includes two of its iconic buildings: the Castelo de São Jorge (St George's Castle) and the Sé (Lisbon Cathedral). Both buildings are worth visiting.

The castle, a Muslim fortress perched on Lisbon's highest hill, offers panoramic views across the city and estuary and was used as a royal residence after the reconquest.

Visiting the cathedral is compulsory as it marks the start of the Camino. The church was constructed on the site of a mosque by its first bishop, a monk and crusader, Gilbert of Hastings. The oldest church in the city and hemmed in by surrounding streets, the building's most striking feature is its façade, with twin crenelated towers and a rose window. When visiting the cathedral be sure to collect your pilgrim's passport.

To learn how funds from the Age of Discovery were spent, visit the Belém Museum District. Located to the west of the city centre, important buildings include the Belém Tower, the Jerónimos Monastery, the Padrão dos Descobrimentos (Monument of the Discoveries), and the Belém Palace. The first two are the most important, and both are UNESCO World Heritage sites. The Tower's design is Muslim-inspired, and its location, originally a small island, served as the disembarkation point for Portuguese explorers and the ceremonial gateway to Lisbon. The Jerónimos Monastery is even more impressive: construction began in 1501 in the Manueline Renaissance style and took 100 years to complete. The building was financed by a 5% tax on the spice trade, the *Vintena da Pimenta*, which produced income equivalent to 70kg of gold per year. It is the home to the tomb of Vasco da Gama. Incidentally, Belém claims that the famous *pastéis de nata* originated at the Pastéis de Belém café.

If after roaming around the Alfama and wondering where the post-earthquake modern urban area happened, then visit Baixa, an elegant district immediately to the west of the Alfama. Here, the previous meandering street pattern was replaced with a grid (now all unidirectional) and employed earthquake-resistant construction, with the buildings' robustness tested by marching troops.

Lisbon is packed with places to eat and drink, including the classic tourist activity of fado and dinner. If there for just one night, then consider the Time Out Mercado da Riberia, Lisbon's primary food market, where canteen-style communal eating allows you to sample different cuisines and drinks from 28 food stalls. If you haven't had one already, try a *ginjinha*, a Lisbon speciality made with a sour-cherry-infused liquor. One will be enough.

Be careful not to follow the blue arrows of the Camino de Fatima (Stage 1 of the Central Camino from Lisbon to Porto)

CAMINO DE FATIMA

Not always helping are another set of arrows, blue ones, waymarks for the Camino de Fatima. Another pilgrimage network, this time descending on the central Portuguese village of Fatima to celebrate the appearances of the Blessed Virgin Mary, Mother of God, to three young peasant children: Francisco, Jacinta, and Lúcia, aged respectively 10, 9, and 7. The Catholic Church has officially recognised the appearances, and the Sanctuary of Our Lady of Fatima is now an international shrine and a major pilgrimage destination. Routes to Fatima, located west of the Central Camino between Santarém and Coimbra, connect from Porto, Lisbon, and Coimbra. The route often, but far from always, coincides with the Camino Portugués, and when you haven't seen a yellow arrow, it's tempting to follow a blue one; this can be a mistake, particularly near Coimbra, where the arrows will send you in the wrong direction.

The Vasco da Gama Tower

STAGE 1

Lisbon to Vila Franca de Xira

Start	Lisbon
Finish	Vila Franca de Xira
Time	3hr
Distance	40km (24.8 miles)
Total ascent	153m
Total descent	153m
Terrain	8km off-road, 32km road

Stage 1 provides a gentle introduction to cycling the Camino. It follows a cycle path out of the city along the Tagus River front, heads inland on a lovely track along the banks of the Rio Trancão, and returns to the Tagus on the final run into Vila Franca de Xira.

Most of the route is on a metalled surface, and apart from one short stretch, the dirt track is also good. The recommended route doesn't follow the Camino out of Lisbon, and leaves it again to avoid a station. If it's early in the season and is at all wet, there is a short section best avoided.

There are many places along the route for a mid-morning coffee and a more substantial lunch.

Vila Franca de Xira has accommodation but little else to commend it. If you can leave Lisbon early, consider cycling all the way to Santarém. If you have arrived in Lisbon by plane and have been to Lisbon before and don't need to see it again, you can join the route east of the airport, near Sacavém, 15km into the route.

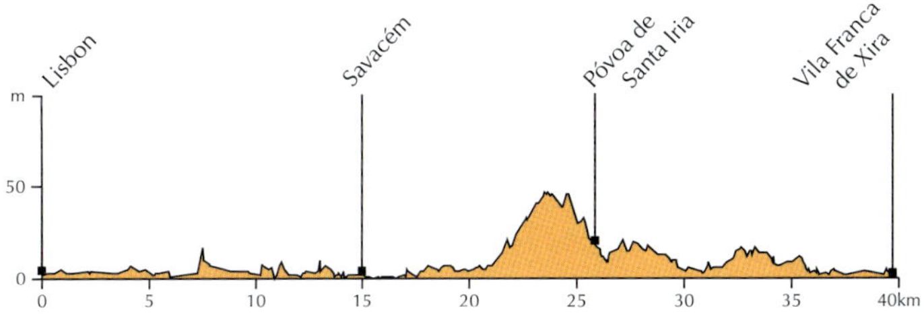

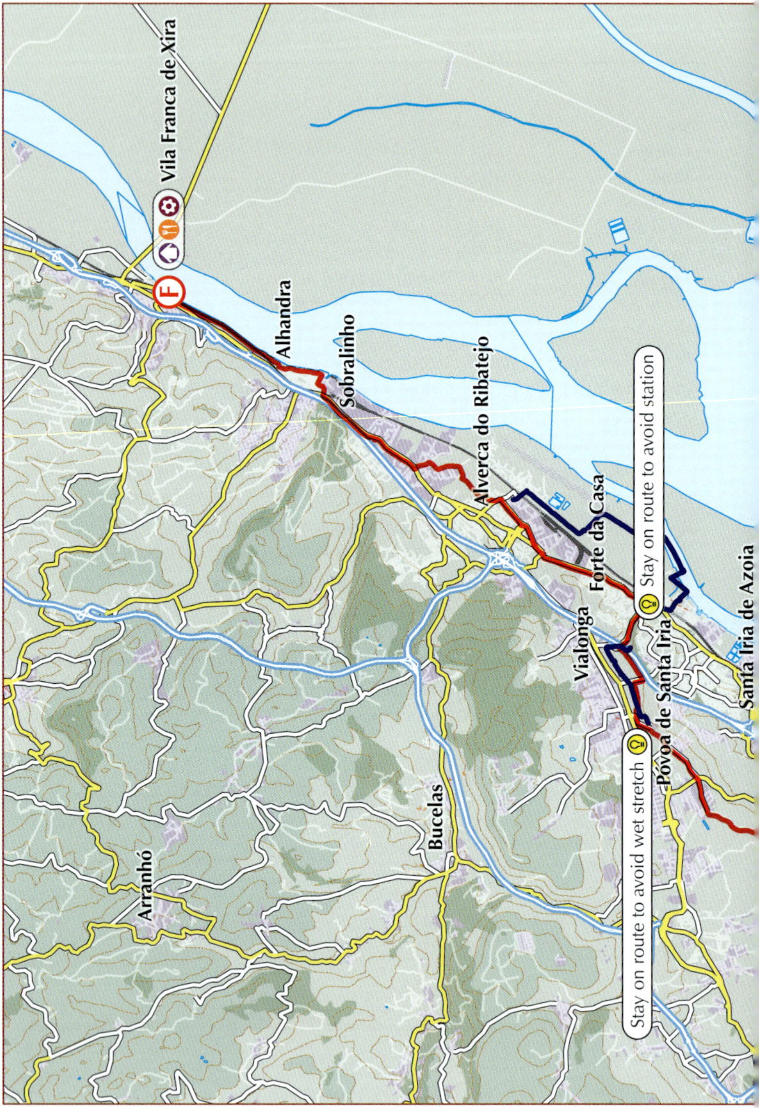
Vila Franca de Xira
Alhandra
Sobralinho
Alverca do Ribatejo
Forte da Casa
Stay on route to avoid station
Vialonga
Póvoa de Santa Iria
Santa Iria de Azoia
Stay on route to avoid wet stretch
Bucelas
Arranhó

N
0
2
4
km
Start of riverside track, avoid if very wet, walk bike if busy
Boardwalk, walk bike if busy
Alcochete
Samouco
Montijo
São João da Talha
Bobadela
Sacavém
Camarate
Póvoa de Santo Adrião
António dos Cavaleiros
Prior Velho
Moscavide
Airport to Camino
Olival Basto
Odivelas
Lisbon

Lisbon to Sacavém 15km

The recommended route starts at Praço do Comércio, a formal square on the riverfront in the centre of Lisbon (with a cycle hire shop on its western side), joining a cycle path heading east and avoiding the stairs, trams, and one-way streets around the cathedral, a near-impossible welcome for any first-time Lisbon cyclist. The first 100m may be busy with tourists and traffic, but once past the ferry terminal, it becomes quieter and follows a cycle path for 8km to Parque das Nações.

The Parque das Nações (Park of Nations) provides a dramatic contrast to Lisbon's historic centre. Built for the World Exhibition in 1998, it features a concentration of modern architecture, including the Lisbon Oceanarium, one of the world's largest; the Science Museum; the Pavilhão do Conhecimento; the Vasco da Gama Tower; and the wave-inspired architecture of the Gare do Oriente station.

At the unmissable Vasco da Gama Tower, the route picks up Camino waymarks, passes beneath the spectacular Vasco da Gama Bridge, and eventually reaches the southern bank of the Rio Trancão in **Sacavém**.

There is a boardwalk on the route before Sacavém, and cycling may not be permitted; if concerned, walk the bike.

Sacavém to Póvoa de Santa Iria 11km

In very wet conditions, the riverside cycle in Sacavém will be muddy and sticky. If it is, stay on the road at Sacavém (the N10) and follow it to **Póvoa de Santa Iria**. Otherwise, enjoy the path, the birds in the river and the flowers. On the approach to Póvoa de Santa Iria, the Camino crosses a very wet water meadow. In all but the driest conditions, use the suggested alternative.

Póvoa de Santa Iria to Vila Franca de Xira 14km

Following the Camino from Póvoa de Santa Iria involves taking bikes through the station at **Alverca do Ribatejo**; to avoid this, the recommended route follows a cycle track for 4km before rejoining the Camino. If you don't mind the station, follow the Camino, which is included as an alternative; it's longer and involves flat off-road cycling, in part through a nature reserve along a boardwalk.

After some mixed urban cycling, the route crosses the railway line, descends to the Tagus, and follows it upstream along a riverside road for 4km into **Vila Franca de Xira**.

Built in 1998, the Vasco da Gama Bridge at 17.2km is the longest in the EU and the second-longest in Europe, after the Crimean Bridge

On the banks of the Rio Trancão

Next home game at Vila Franca de Xira

VILA FRANCA DE XIRA

Vila Franca de Xira is blighted by traffic and feels run-down and neglected. It has accommodation, a few places to eat, and a good bike shop that serves coffee. It also provides an introduction to the bull-running (*touradas*) tradition (in which bulls are apparently not killed), which features in all towns and villages throughout the Ribatejo. The highlight is the Colete Encardo, the Red Vest Festival, which takes place in July, where *campino* (cowboys) perform daring feats.

For non-hostel accommodation, the Hospedaria Maioral is the best bet in town, but it's very small and often fully booked. The Leziria Parque Hotel is larger, near the route, but outside the town to the north. Both hotels have restaurants and serve breakfast. There are also two hostels, both with private rooms.

There is a choice of restaurants, particularly traditional Portuguese heavy on meat and fish for example, 150 Gramas or Restaurante – O Galo da Vila. There are also several Asian restaurants with a bigger choice of vegetarian dishes, for example, the Masala, which is close to the Hospedaria Maiora.

Vila Franca de Xira – home of touradas

STAGE 2

Vila Franca de Xira to Santarém

Start	Vila Franca de Xira
Finish	Santarém
Time	4hr
Distance	53km (32.9 miles)
Total ascent	121m
Total descent	23m
Terrain	6km off-road, 47km road

If you share my interest in vegetables and intensive agriculture, you'll enjoy Stage 2; if you don't, then the abiding memory will be: the flat, easy cycling; the pretty riverside town of Valeda; and the sting in the tail, the final climb up to Santerém. Either way, after a mixed, but essentially urban Stage 1, Stage 2 will feel like an escape.

The main challenge is navigating the railway stations, and the recommended route avoids all three. Apart from a farm track near the beginning, nearly all the cycling is along flat, metalled roads. There are good coffee places in Vila Nova da Rainha and Azambuja, and Valada, a lovely riverside village with swimming opportunities, is an ideal place for lunch.

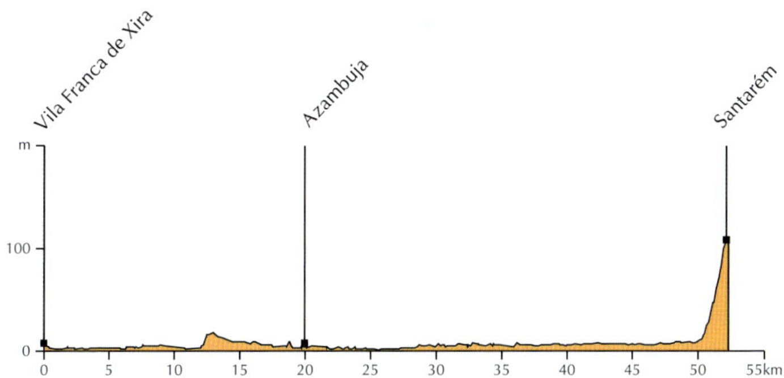

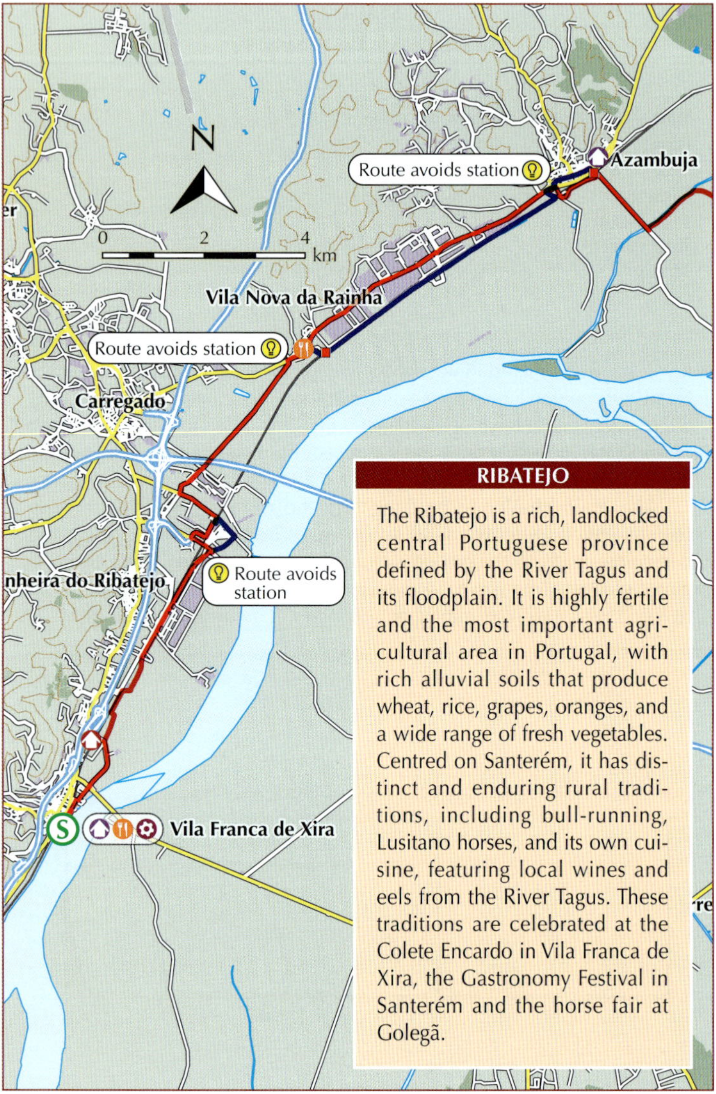

RIBATEJO

The Ribatejo is a rich, landlocked central Portuguese province defined by the River Tagus and its floodplain. It is highly fertile and the most important agricultural area in Portugal, with rich alluvial soils that produce wheat, rice, grapes, oranges, and a wide range of fresh vegetables. Centred on Santerém, it has distinct and enduring rural traditions, including bull-running, Lusitano horses, and its own cuisine, featuring local wines and eels from the River Tagus. These traditions are celebrated at the Colete Encardo in Vila Franca de Xira, the Gastronomy Festival in Santerém and the horse fair at Golegã.

Vila Franca de Xira to Azambuja 19.8km

The recommended route leaves the Camino three times to avoid three stations. The first one involves following the road over the railway line and around to the other side of the station. Whether or not to avoid the second one is a more marginal decision. The recommended route avoids the station but follows the hard shoulder for 6km on a busy main road. Avoiding the busy road involves carrying bikes over a footbridge, but the station is very quiet, as is the track used by the Camino on the other side. The third station is busy, and although the lifts are operational, getting through the station is an unpleasant experience. Avoiding the station, however, means missing **Azambuja**.

Azambuja to Santerém 33.2km

Leaving Azambuja and the railway line behind, the Camino escapes into flat, productive agricultural land reminiscent of the fens in the east of England. The recommended route follows the Camino all the way to Santerém (sticking to the road underneath the flood prevention dykes rather than the narrow track on top of them).

Valada, a one-street village running parallel to the Tagus, is a stopover for walking pilgrims and offers plenty of places for coffee, including a riverside restaurant where, depending on the season, you can watch locals swim in the river.

Flat land on the approach to Santarém

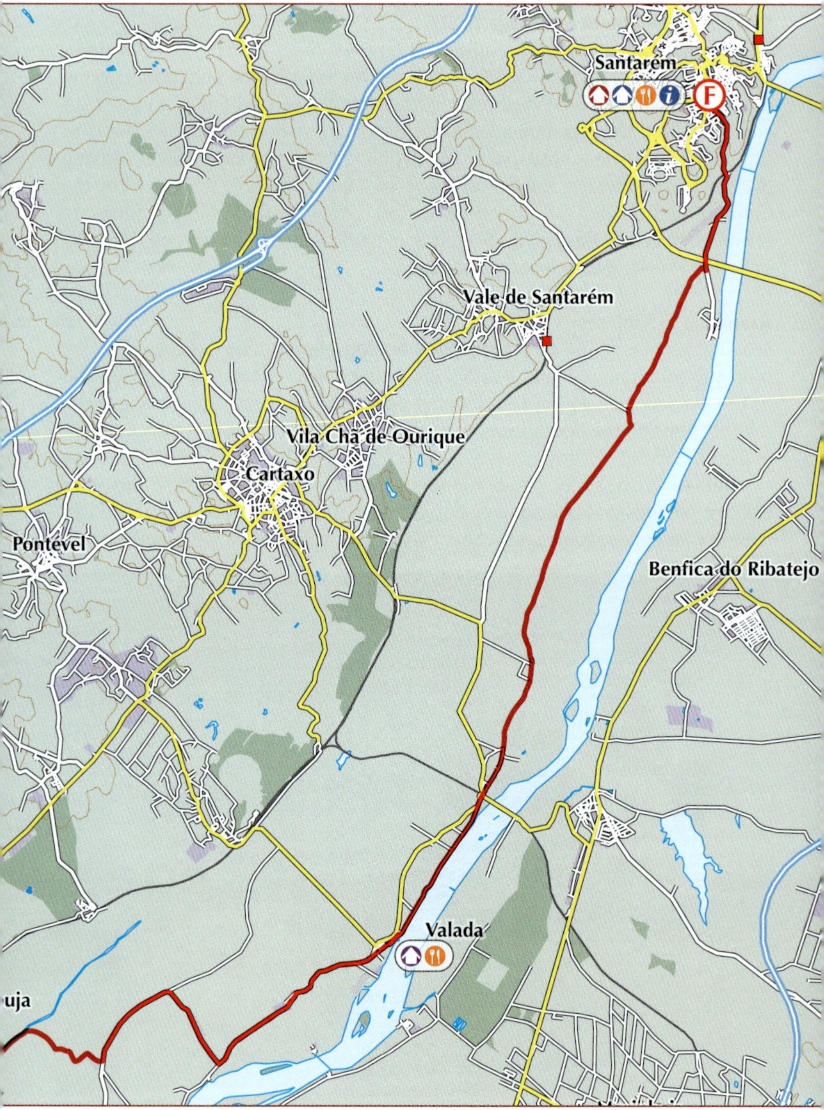
Santarém
F
Vale de Santarém
Vila Chã de Ourique
Cartaxo
Pontevel
Benfica do Ribatejo
Valada
uja

SANTERÉM

Santarém, perched on a promontory overlooking the River Tagus, has a strong defensive position. From the Romans onward, successive rulers of Portugal recognised its potential and invested in its fortifications. It was the staging post for the reconquest of Lisbon in 1147 and the starting point for the military coup in 1974 (the Carnation Revolution), which ended the dictatorship and marked the beginning of democracy.

Despite being damaged in the 1755 earthquake, it has the largest ensemble of Gothic churches in Portugal. There is a lot to see, but the old town is compact and easy to get around. Definitely worth visiting are: the Jardim Portas do Sol, a Muslim castle with great views over the Tagus; the Church of Santa Maria de Marvila, built by the Knights Templar in 1149; the Sanctuary of the Eucharist Miracle of Santerém (a notable miracle story); and the richly decorated Santerém Cathedral.

There is plenty of accommodation and, depending on the time of year, good places to eat. The best non-hostel place to stay is A Casa Brava – it's in the old part of town and has good bike storage. As well as traditional Portuguese restaurants, Santerém has a fine dining option at Ó Balcão, a Michelin-star restaurant specialising in river fish (booking ahead recommended); a really interesting Peruvian/Japanese fusion restaurant with outdoor eating at Restaurante Pátio da Graça; and a healthy food restaurant with good vegetarian options at Eva Pecado Natural. Make sure you have a drink before dinner in the main square; it is a lovely place to watch the sun go down.

Saint Francis Borgia in the Santerém Cathedral, skull in hand

Blue sky, blue building

STAGE 3

Santerém to Tomar

Start	Santerém
Finish	Tomar
Time	4hr 40min
Distance	64km (39.8 miles)
Total ascent	304m
Total descent	363m
Terrain	40km road, 24km off-road

Tomar is still in the Ribatejo, but Stage 3 makes the transition from a landscape dominated by the River Tagus and its vast, intensively farmed floodplain to one covered in trees, hillier, and, from a cycling perspective, more interesting. The flat cycling continues for the first two-thirds of the route, with the final third off-road on an undulating forest track. Tomar is a fantastic destination with much to see, and its attractions make a good excuse to avoid the more challenging cycling and take a direct route.

Azinhaga, the birthplace of Nobel laureate José Saramago, is a pretty village, an obvious place to stop for a mid-morning coffee. There are many lunchtime options in Golegã, but if it's too early, consider Vila Nova da Barquinha.

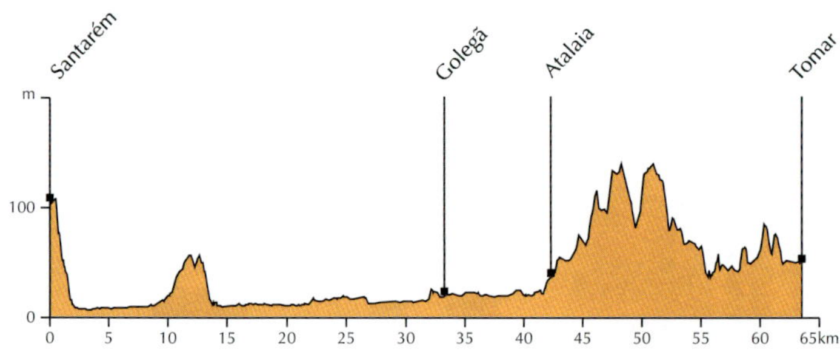

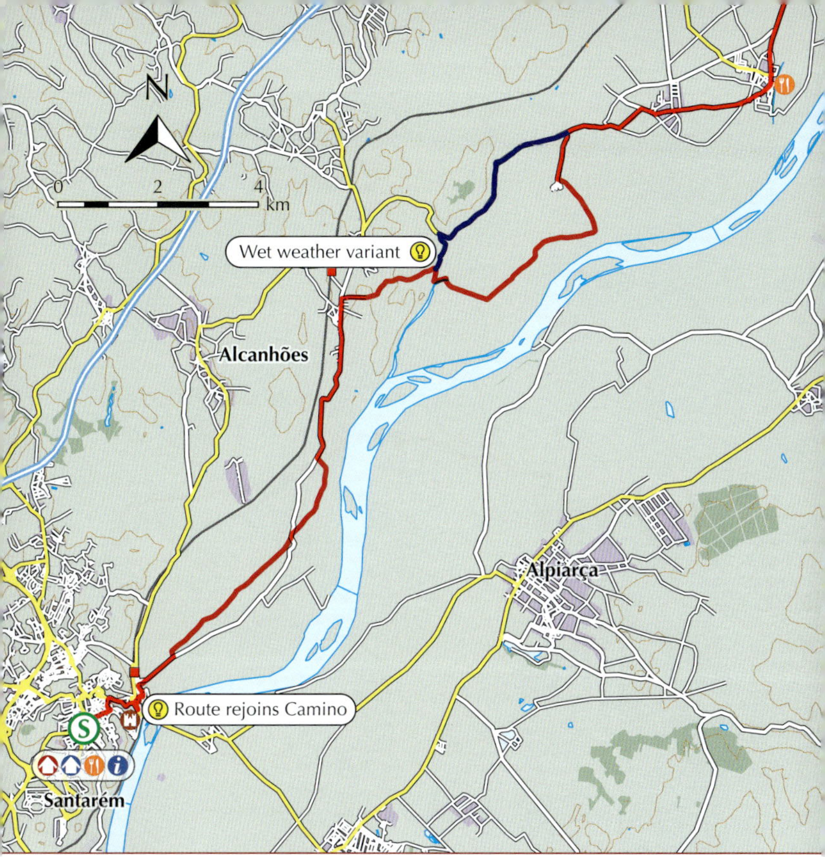

Tomar Castle from the old town

Spring planting in the Ribatejo

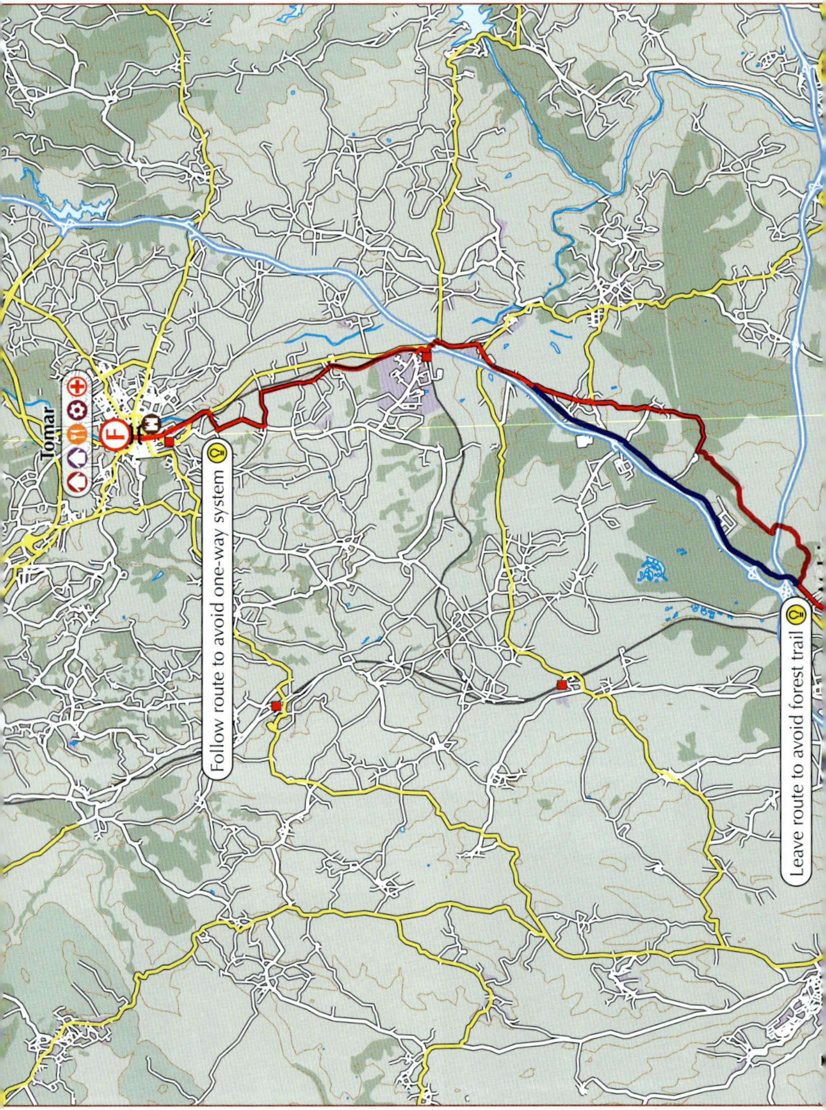
Tomar
Follow route to avoid one-way system
Leave route to avoid forest trail

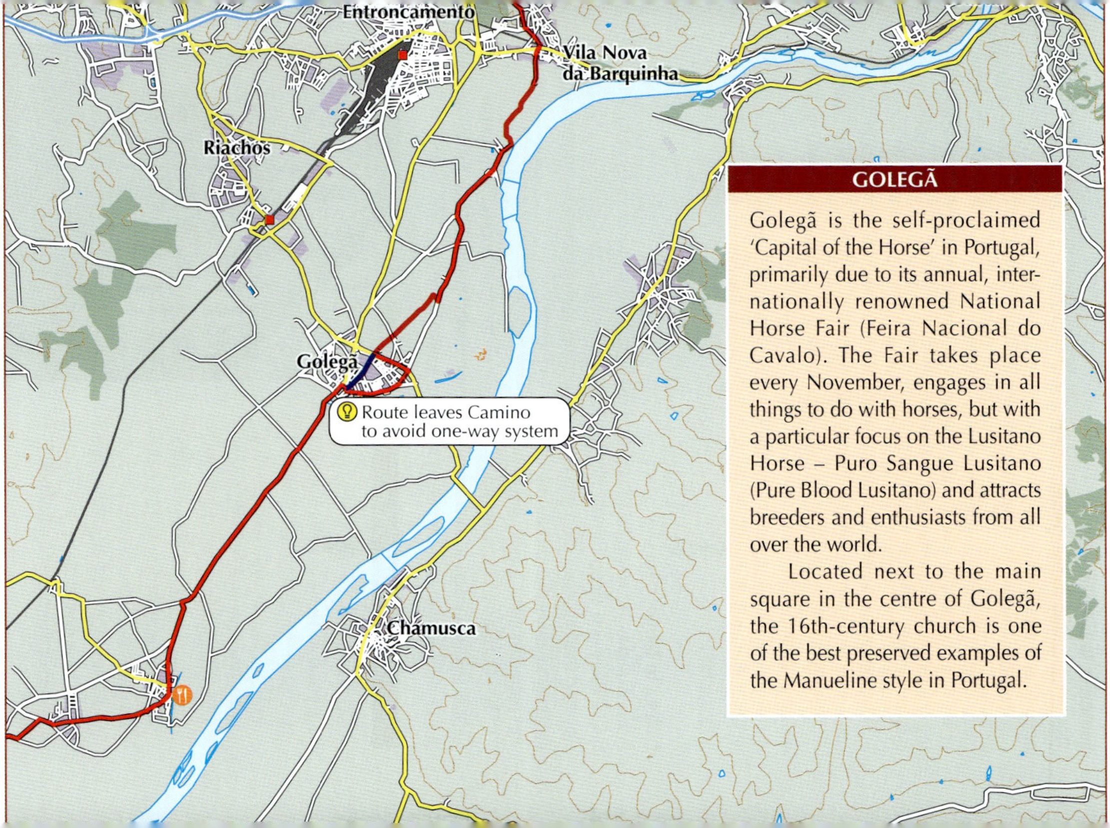

GOLEGÃ

Golegã is the self-proclaimed 'Capital of the Horse' in Portugal, primarily due to its annual, internationally renowned National Horse Fair (Feira Nacional do Cavalo). The Fair takes place every November, engages in all things to do with horses, but with a particular focus on the Lusitano Horse – Puro Sangue Lusitano (Pure Blood Lusitano) and attracts breeders and enthusiasts from all over the world.

Located next to the main square in the centre of Golegã, the 16th-century church is one of the best preserved examples of the Manueline style in Portugal.

Santerém to Golegã 33km

The waymarking in the countryside north of Santerém is confusing, so you may need to rely on GPS.

The first challenge is getting out of Santerém. The Camino follows a steep path, unsuitable for bikes, down from the castle at the eastern end of the town; instead, the recommended route descends to a road to the north before rejoining the Camino at the bottom of the hill. It then heads out into the countryside following a mix of roads and agricultural tracks. After 12km, the route turns right and heads towards the Tagus. If it's a wet season or there has been recent rain, the route will be waterlogged and impassable; therefore, take the alternative route.

The recommended route leaves the Camino at Golegã to avoid the town's one-way system.

After experiencing the first sustained stretch of Portugal's famous cobbled road on the approach to the town, walking through the city might be the preferred approach.

Golegã to Tomar 31km

From **Atalaia**, the route heads up to a main road, then turns right onto a forest track. There is a steep initial climb, then a descent to a footbridge over a motorway and then another short but very steep climb. Recent forest clearing has made the ground along the undulating trail very soft. If it's really wet, consider taking the alternative route to Tomar, it will be empty.

The Camino follows an old railway line on the final approach to **Tomar**, with a short stretch closed to cyclists. The recommended route follows the detour and leaves the Camino upon entering the town to avoid the one-way system.

QUINTA CARDIGA

On the banks of the Tagus, just beyond Golegã, is the Quinta Cardiga, a fascinating set of buildings, many overgrown with ivy, through which peeps a lovely pink façade. The buildings date back to the Knights Templar and in the core of the complex is a Renaissance palace. Unfortunately, the buildings are inaccessible but there are plans to restore them as a luxury hotel.

Quinta Cardiga

The main square in Tomar

TOMAR

Tomar is a lovely historic town located on the banks of the River Nabão founded within the walls of the Convent of Christ and Tomar Castle, built by the Knights Templar and serving as their headquarters. The Knights Templar were a vast crusading organisation that played a crucial role in the Reconquest but were banned elsewhere in Europe from 1312. In Portugal, the Knights Templar was rebranded as the Order of Christ and its wealth and influence grew under Henry the Navigator, who became its grand master. The Order's cross adorned the sails of the Portuguese caravel ships, the technical development of which facilitated the Age of Discovery.

The Convent of Christ, a UNESCO World Heritage Site, is located above the town and can be reached via a footpath. With construction starting in 1160 and continuing for five centuries, the building complex showcases a mix of styles including Romanesque, Gothic, Manueline, and Renaissance. The standout features are the 12th-century Templar Rotunda, a circular (12-sided) church (modelled on the Church of the Holy Sepulchre in Jerusalem) where knights on horseback could attend Mass; and the Manueline window in the Chapter House whose intricate maritime carvings – ropes, corals, and the cross of the Order of Christ – symbolise Portugal's Age of Discovery and naval power.

The old town sits below the convent and features, next to the chequerboard-tiled main square, the Church of St John the Baptist, with an impressive Gothic façade and portal, and a tower with a 16th-century clock. Nearby is a medieval synagogue, the only one left in Portugal and it was closed in 1496 following the expulsion of the Jews.

Tomar has a good choice of accommodation at different price points. Staying in the old town on the left-hand side of the river provides good access to the sights and restaurants, but accommodation on the right-hand side offers excellent views of Tomar Castle. The old town is definitely the best place to eat. Head to the main square, have a pre-dinner drink and have a look at the menu at the Taverna Antiqua. It's a medieval-themed restaurant, with vegetarian options, and you can sit outside.

Ponte Romana da Portagem in Tomar is the first of many medieval bridges on the Camino built on Roman foundations.

Convent of Christ and Tomar Castle

STAGE 4

Tomar to Ansião

Start	Tomar
Finish	Ansião
Time	4hr 10min
Distance	47km (29.2 miles)
Total ascent	767m
Total descent	608m
Terrain	40km metalled, 7km off-road

Stage 4 is just 47km long but includes challenging cycling, featuring the route's most significant climb between Lisbon and Porto. It's also very quiet, passing through remote empty countryside and, if the recommended route is adopted, uses empty country roads with a reasonable surface. Ansião is a small town with few attractions, so there is no need to rush. If the weather is good, there is a charming place for a picnic stop. It's next to a millpond in the forest with apparent (untested) wild-swimming potential.

Mid-morning coffee can be found at Calvinos (12km), and if you don't go al fresco, take lunch at Alvaiázere (34km) just before the main climb.

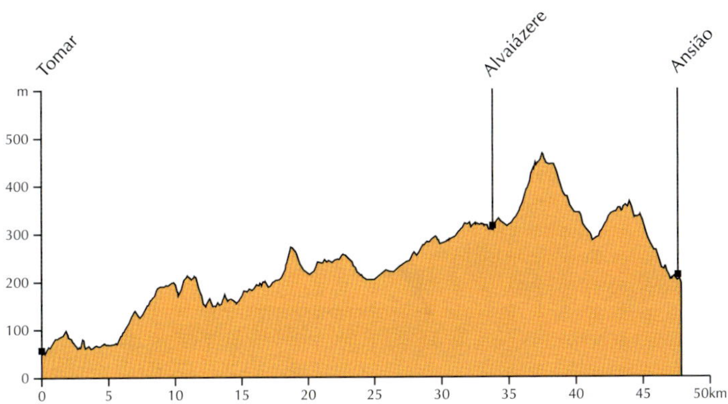

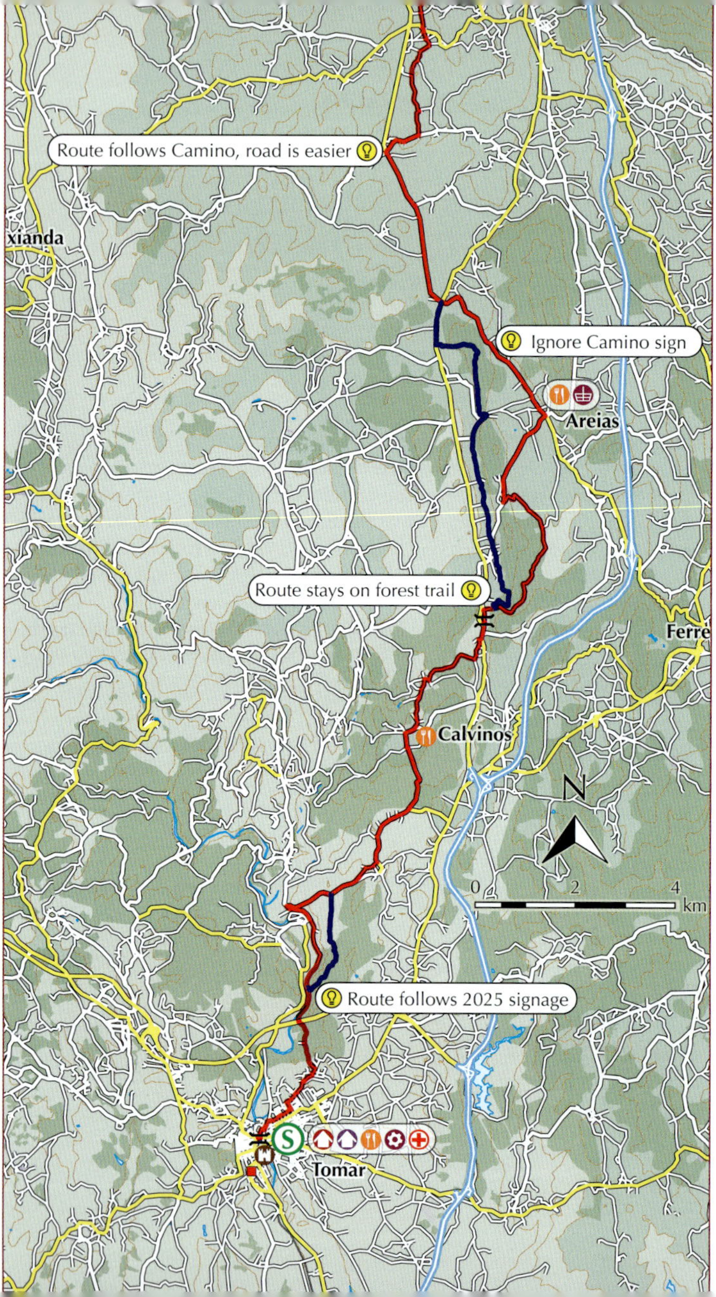

Route follows Camino, road is easier
xianda
Ignore Camino sign
Areias
Route stays on forest trail
Ferre
Calvinos
N
0
2
4
km
Route follows 2025 signage
S
Tomar

Tomar to Alvaiázere 33.7km

The route leaving Tomar has recently changed, and new waymarks have been installed. To navigate a one-way system, the recommended route deviates from the Camino by about 200m. There was also a 2025 route change just beyond the point where the route passes under the motorway. The recommended route follows the 2025 signage but the official route is also shown on the map.

There are two Camino options in the forest just beyond the Ponte de Ceras, and the recommended route continues on the forest road avoiding a very steep climb. The picnic spot is just beyond the point where the route splits. There is another potential coffee stop in the village of **Areias**.

The worst road surface is on the approach to **Alvaiázere**, about 6km south of the town. The Camino and recommended route turn right off the Estrada Caminho de Santiago and head north on a meandering route through a series of tiny villages, some with cobbles. Staying on the Estrada is a tempting alternative.

Alvaiázere is a small town with a full range of facilities, including chemists, ATMs, general stores and several cafés and restaurants.

Alvaiázere to Ansião 13.3km

Leaving Alvaiázere, the route makes its most significant climb to date, but it's just 150m, and the ascent is steady. The small village of Vendas is just beyond the pass. On the descent to **Ansião**, the recommended route avoids some challenging singletrack and a one-way street on the final approach to the town.

ANSIÃO

Ansião offers a full range of local services and shops, but nothing particularly noteworthy to visit. There are two hotels, a hostel run by the fire service and some room-only options. One of the hotels is well located, very comfortable and appears to be operated by the local authority. The other is a hotel/restaurant which, given the limited restaurant choice in Ansião, is an attraction.

A Portuguese hórreo

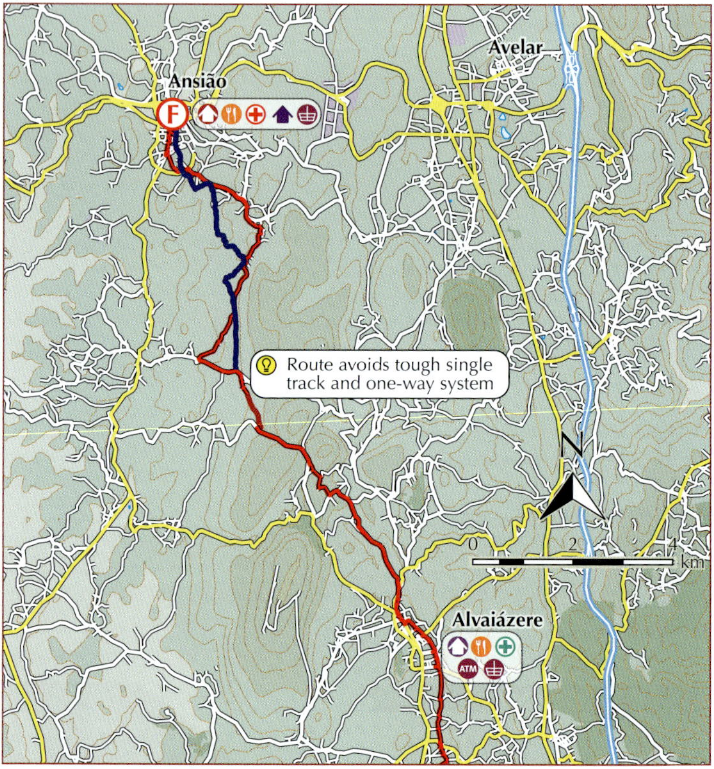

Swimming in a mill pond?

Breakfast and the lottery at Ansião

STAGE 5

Ansião to Coimbra

Start	Ansião
Finish	Coimbra
Time	4hr
Distance	47km (29.2 miles)
Ascent	530m
Descent	714m
Terrain	26km road, 21km off-road

Stage 5 is the same length as Stage 4, passes through the same remote, hilly landscape and presents some similar challenges. It's all potentially cyclable, but there is a lot more undulating off-road cycling, some of which cyclists who aren't off-road confident might want to avoid. The recommended route avoids the worst bits. The good news is that alternative routes are easy to identify, and the roads at this stage are empty.

The route includes a visit to the Roman ruins at Conímbriga. It's worth allowing time for a walk around the site and, if time permits, a visit to the associated museum and restaurant.

For a mid-morning break, consider Alvorge or Rabaçal – at Rabaçal, you can sample a distinct and very nice local cheese.

If you need a break from cycling on the way to Porto, Coimbra is the best place to stop.

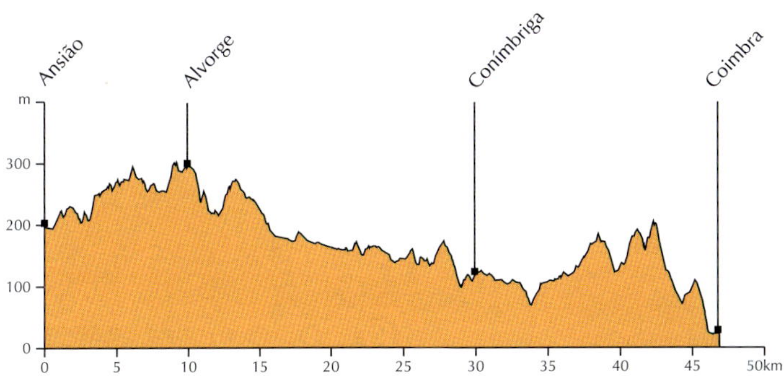

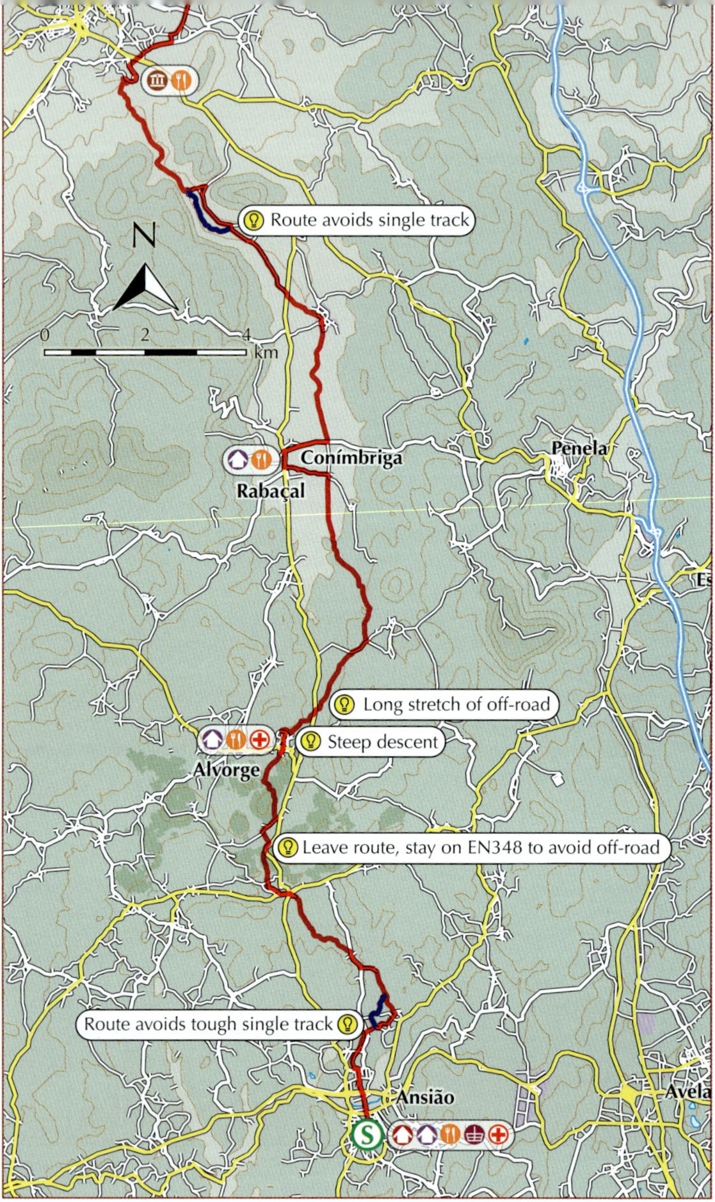
Route avoids single track
N
0
2
4
km
Conímbriga
Rabaçal
Penela
Long stretch of off-road
Steep descent
Alvorge
Leave route, stay on EN348 to avoid off-road
Route avoids tough single track
Ansião
S

Ansião to Conímbriga 29.5km
To avoid a stretch of rocky single track and carrying your bike, leave the Camino after 2.3km and rejoin it 1km later.

The cycling either side of **Alvorge** has some challenges. There is a short but steep descent from the road onto a track (7.7km); a steep descent on leaving Alvorge (10.5km); and a long climb across heath on a rocky track (11.5km), which not everyone will enjoy. To avoid these hazards, stay on the main road, EN348 (it should be empty), bypass Alvorge, and continue to **Rabaçal** for coffee and cheese.

The only deviation from the Camino occurs at 24.5km, where the recommended route stays on the road, avoiding a very narrow single track that runs perilously close to a stream.

RABAÇAL

Rabaçal cheese (*queijo Rabaçal*) is a traditional Portuguese semi-hard cheese unique to the Coimbra region. It's made from a blend of ewe's and goat's milk with a distinct flavour derived from the local thyme pastures recently visited by the Camino. It's enjoyed with bread, nuts, honey, or sweet brandies, but works well with a mid-morning coffee, too.

Cheesy mid-morning break at Rabaçal

Conímbriga to Coimbra 17.5km

As it approaches Coimbra, the Camino gets quite close to the A1, Portugal's main motorway; it's more built-up, and navigation is more complicated (the blue pilgrim signs going the wrong way are particularly misleading). Despite this, the Camino follows a route with off-road and rural elements. The recommended route misses **Cernache**, whose one-way street is the wrong way. The final descent into **Coimbra**, from the top of the hill with amazing views, is very steep

CONÍMBRIGA

Conímbriga is one of the largest and best-preserved Roman settlements excavated in Portugal and was a significant urban centre in the Roman province of Lusitania.

Remains include a 1500m-long defensive wall, its main gate, and well-preserved private houses, including the Casa dos Repuxos (House of the Fountains). Particularly notable are the intricate polychromatic mosaics that cover many floors, depicting mythological scenes and geometric patterns. The onsite museum provides information on the site's history and displays artefacts found during excavations. The scale of the remains is even more impressive given that an estimated 85% are unexcavated.

Mosaic at Conímbriga

The cloisters in the Coimbra Cathedral

COIMBRA

With Roman, Visigothic and Muslim antecedents, Coimbra is famous for its university, founded in 1290, one of the oldest in Europe and is known as the 'city of students'.

The university buildings, awarded UNESCO World Heritage designation in 2013, sit atop a hill and are surrounded by a square overlooking the Mondego River. The most important buildings are the Paço das Escolas (Royal Palace of Alcáçova), once the residence of Portuguese kings, which includes the Sala dos Capelos (Great Hall of Acts) and the iconic Torre da Universidade (Baroque University Tower), whose bells still regulate academic life. The Joanina Library is a stunning 18th-century Baroque library whose books are protected from insects by a colony of bats (let out every night). The Capela de São Miguel (São Miguel Chapel), a Manueline-style chapel adjacent to the library, houses a magnificent 18th-century Baroque organ.

Also significant, but not part of the university, is Sé Velha, the Romanesque old cathedral (there is also newer one), a fortress-like church with Gothic cloisters, and the Monastery of Santa Cruz (Mosteiro de Santa Cruz), founded in 1131 and the burial place of Portugal's first two kings, Afonso Henriques and Sancho I. Particularly striking is the portal and façade which, if you get to see it in evening sunlight, shows off Coimbra's distinctive yellowish limestone.

If staying for more than one night, visit the Machado de Castro National Museum, rated as one of Portugal's most important museums.

For a tour of the town starting from the west side of the river have a quick look at the Mosteiro de Santa Clara-a-Velha, a site central to the Pedro and Inês story below, then take the footbridge over the river (just a little upstream), walk up through the botanical gardens, leave near the aqueduct (built in 1570), and head into the University complex. After exploring the buildings, head down and visit the Old Cathedral. Just below the Cathedral, in a narrow, pedestrianised street, enjoy well-deserved refreshments and take in some Fado at the Fado Centre. Returning down the hill from the Fado Centre, pass through the old city gates, one of which, the Porta e Torre de Almedina, is a pre-Reconquest Muslim construction.

Coimbra is a dense, hilly place, so choose accommodation that is readily accessible. Exit for Stage 6 heads north (or left as you face the city) along a cycle path near the bridge. There are two hotels worth considering on the west side of the River and two near the station. The Guest House Santa Clara, is particularly nice – great views but you need to keep your bike with you in your room. The hostel is great value, but harder to get to. Incidentally, there is a lot of poor accommodation in Coimbra.

Coimbra skyline in the evening

Barriga de friera, "nun's belly"

FOOD AND DRINK

There are a wide variety of restaurants in Coimbra, but it is particularly proud of its craft beers, with several microbreweries and bars specialising in artisan ales. The Cervejaria Praxis is suitable for beer and food but is not in the old town, whereas the Oak Food Beer & Wine restaurant is and offers good vegetarian options.

Try a *barriga de freira* (nun's belly), a local dessert made with egg yolks, sugar and bread.

PEDRO AND INÊS

Coimbra is the setting for Portugal's most famous and tragic romance. Prince Pedro, the son and heir to King Afonso IV, fell in love with Inês, his wife's lady-in-waiting, much to his father's disapproval. After his wife died, they lived together in Coimbra and had children. The King, fearful of Inês's influence, had her assassinated, and, heartbroken and vengeful, Pedro led a rebellion against his father. When he ascended to the throne after two years, he captured the two assassins and had their hearts ripped out, one through the front and one through the back. Pedro had Inês's decomposing body exhumed, crowned in a coronation, and all the nobles had to kiss her decomposing hand. Today, Pedro and Inês rest in the Monastery of Alcobaça in tombs facing each other so that, on Judgement Day, they will see one another immediately.

STAGE 6

Coimbra to Albergaria-a-Velha

Start	Coimbra
Finish	Albergaria-a-Velha
Time	5hr
Distance	65km (40.4 miles)
Total ascent	504m
Total descent	403m
Terrain	55km road, 10km off-road

Stage 6 presents a mixed bag of cycling, combining quiet country roads, easy off-road cycling through eucalyptus forests, small towns (all with Muslim-derived names), and some large, ugly industrial estates.

Aside from minor deviations to avoid one-way streets, the recommended route follows the Camino to Albergaria-a-Velha. There are three short but easy climbs, but the main challenge is navigating the three medium-sized towns along the route, Mealhada, Anadia and Águeda, all of which have confusing one-way systems. Mealhada has plenty of places for a mid-morning coffee, and Águeda is an obvious lunch stop.

Albergaria-a-Vela, halfway between Coimbra and Póvoa de Varzim, is a poor stopover, with limited accommodation and little to see. It's the only place on the route to Porto where booking ahead is essential. Águeda is a more interesting town and has a better choice of accommodation and places to eat. It's 50km from Coimbra (rather than 65km) and adds around an hour to the journey to Porto, but it is worth considering as an alternative stopover if you are happy with the extra distance on the final stage.

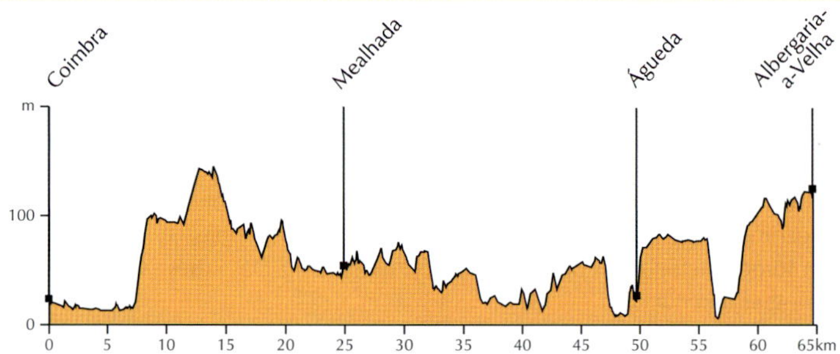

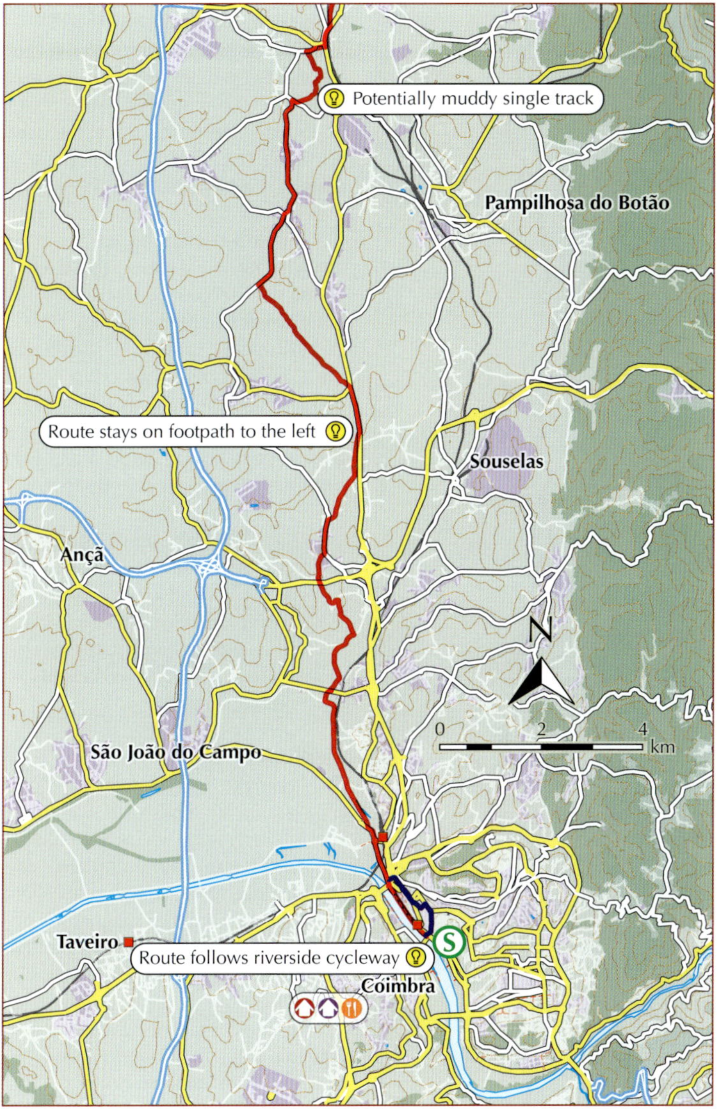
Potentially muddy single track
Pampilhosa do Botão
Route stays on footpath to the left
Souselas
Ançã
N
0
2
4
km
São João do Campo
Taveiro
S
Route follows riverside cycleway
Coimbra

Coimbra to Mealhada 25km

The Camino wanders through the centre of hilly Coimbra. For a much easier exit, the recommended route heads north along the right bank of the river, rejoining the Camino after passing under a road bridge. After 11.9km on the Camino, it joins a main road, with the Camino remaining on the hard shoulder but on the wrong side. Cycling on the hard shoulder is uncomfortable, but it avoids two road crossings.

Just before arriving in Mealhada, the Camino crosses an olive grove/orchard, and the track may be muddy after heavy rain. At **Mealhada**, there is a short deviation to avoid a one-way on a partially pedestrianised street.

Mealhada feels run-down but has a good range of services, lots of cafés and a bike shop. If stopping for coffee in Mealhada, stay on the Camino. Apparently, Mealhada is the place in Portugal to eat suckling pig.

Mealhada to Águeda 25km

The cycling to Águeda is 'mixed', combining rural stretches with warehousing. Just be grateful you're not walking.

The square on the northern side of the bridge at Águeda is an excellent place for lunch and a magnet for pilgrims recovering from a walk through an industrial estate (definitely better by bike).

To avoid the one-way system in **Águeda**, leave the Camino and rejoin to the north of the town centre.

Agueda Umbrella Sky Project (Photo by Tormius)

ÁGUEDA

The town has a full range of services, hostels, hotels, restaurants and a very popular bike shop. Its main claim to fame, however, is the Umbrella Sky Project, which runs each year between July and September (and the run-up to Christmas), and involves a colourful canopy of umbrellas that creates a shady open-air art gallery, an idea now copied around the world. Águeda is proud of its municipal art, which adorns a number of its buildings.

If Águeda is the preferred stopover, there is accommodation at the Hotel Conde de Águeda and two hostels both with private rooms. The Manjar da Helena, located near the river, appears to be the best restaurant, although its opening hours are restricted during the off-season.

Street art in Águeda

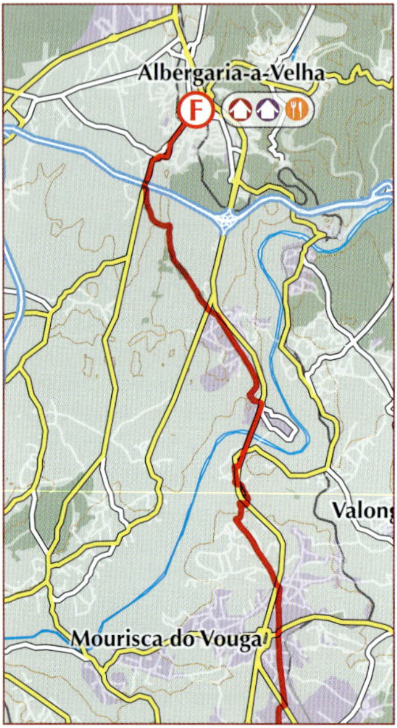

Eucalyptus on the approach to Albergaria-a-Velha

Águeda to Albergaria-a-Velha 15km

After visiting the lovely medieval bridge, the Ponte Velha do Marnel, the route crosses the River Vouga and turns left up a steep hill on the other side. It's a busy road, and crossing the traffic needs care.

There is very little to see in **Albergaria-a-Velha**, few places to eat and only two places to stay. There is pilgrim-style accommodation at the Restaurant Parente: simple rooms with shared bathrooms, but fun, or self-catering accommodation in smarter rooms just around the corner at UP Estalagem dos Padres.

Ponte Velha do Marnel

STAGE 7

Albergaria-a-Velha to Porto

Start	Albergaria-a-Velha
Finish	Porto
Time	5hr 40min
Distance	71.2km (44.2 miles)
Total ascent	782m
Total descent	894m
Terrain	58km road (or cobbles), 13.2km off-road

There is no sugar-coating it: Stage 7 is the worst day on the entire Camino Portugués. Although there are a few stretches of quiet rural cycling, the overwhelming impression will be one of urban sprawl. The route is complex, with numerous junctions and turns that make navigation challenging. Adding to the frustration of missed turns, the share of streets with cobbled surfaces increases.

The distance includes 7km riding along the cycle path to the western side of Porto and assumes the recommendation to stay outside the city's busy central area is accepted.

To avoid heading the wrong way up one-way streets, the recommended route makes several detours, some very minor. The main detour is on the approach to Porto, at Perosinho, where the recommended route leaves the Camino, skipping a steep climb along a challenging, stepped track and significant bike carrying. The recommended route includes a 400m stretch of Roman road whose surface has deteriorated since Roman times.

The final run into Porto follows a busy road shared with the new metro system, which runs along the centre of a dual carriageway and over the city's famous Dom Luís bridge. Although it's tempting to cross the bridge on the top level (amazing views), the recommended route heads down to the Douro on the south side. After passing under the bridge, turn sharply right, then cross the bridge on the lower deck. On the north side, head west, walk through the crowds, and, once it's clear enough, continue on the road/cycle track.

There are plenty of places to stop for coffee and lunch, and try the local speciality, the francesinha.

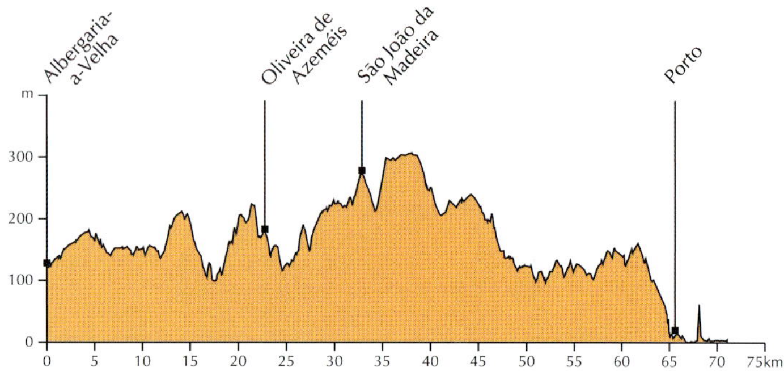

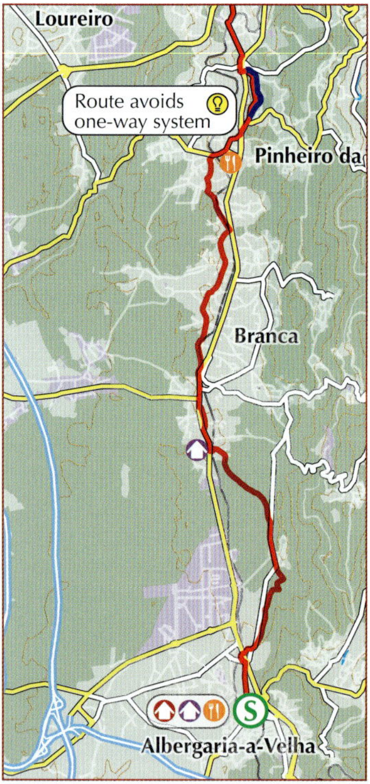

Albergaria-a-Velha to São João da Madeira 32km

After navigating the one-way system out of Albergaria-a-Velha, the route stays on the Camino (it might be a bit early, but the Restaurant Vouguinha, an old railway station (12.4km), is a lovely coffee place) until another one-way system forces a short detour (13.1km). There is another one-way street with an enforced detour (19.1km) on the approach to the busy town of **Oliveira de Azeméis**, and another that takes you through the city itself (20km).

São João da Madeira (22,000) is an important industrial town near Portugal's main motorway, known for its shoe industry. If you don't find the navigation and traffic too stressful, there are plenty of places to stop for refreshments.

São João da Madeira to Porto 39.2km

There are four minor variations of the Camino between **São João da Madeira** and Perosinho, all to avoid one-way streets and to navigate the motorway network south of Porto. At **Perosinho**, the recommended route turns left (54.7km) and then right, after 1km, through the **Canelas** before rejoining the Camino and the route into **Porto.**

Francesinha – Porto's favourite

FRANCESINHA

On my first trip to Porto, the café owner suggested we try the city's traditional dish, the *francesinha*. What a strange dish. Essentially, it features toasted sliced white bread (a classic English sliced loaf style) with a ham and cheese filling (other meats are used), blanketed in melted cheese and covered in a rich sauce (gravy). We thought we had made a mistake, but once in Porto, we discovered that it's something locals can't get enough of.

Porto
F
Fânzeres
São
Gondomar
Route avoids central Porto
Valbom
Vila Nova de Gaia
Madalena
Avintes
Valadares
Canelas
Carvalhos
Route avoids difficult single track
Olival
Perosinho
Arcozelo
Serzedo
N
São Félix da Marinha
Grijó
0
2
4
km
Argoncilhe
Espinho
Anta
Nogueira da Regedoura
Route avoids one-way system
Fiães
Silvalde
São Paio de Oleiros
Lourosa
Santa Maria de Lamas
Paços de Brandão
Esmoriz
Rio Meão
São João de Ver
ATM

Porto cathedral dominates the skyline

Azulejo tiles

PORTO

Initially a Celtic and later a Roman settlement, Porto became the cornerstone of the county, then the Kingdom, of Portugal after its capture from the Muslims in 868. It's located on the northern side of the River Douro, opposite its smaller sister city, Vila Nova de Gaia, on the southern side. It enjoys a spectacular location, 3km inland from the Atlantic, in a narrow gorge enhanced by the double-decked Dom Luís I Bridge, from which you can enjoy some of the best views of the city.

The heart of the city is the Ribeira district. The Ribeira district includes the riverfront west of the Dom Luis I Bridge, the streets leading up to the Cathedral, the Cathedral, and Ribeira Square itself. The district holds UNESCO World Heritage Site status, and its narrow streets, with tall, multicoloured houses, are built for strolling (not cycling).

Gustave Eiffel didn't design the Dom Luis I Bridge; he lost the 1880 construction competition to his former partner, the German Théophile Seyrig. Théophile was also responsible for the similarly looking Maria Pia Bridge, just up the river.

In addition to its bridge and iconic location, the colour of its glazed tiles (*azulejos*) is a defining feature of Porto. They are everywhere. The classic colour scheme is blue and white (inspired by Delftware-style designs from Holland). Although they are a symbol of wealth, they also help resist the effects of Atlantic weather. Perhaps the best place to see them is São Bento Railway Station. The entrance hall is covered with approximately 20,000 tiles by artist Jorge Colaço, depicting scenes from Portuguese history.

Not to be outdone by its bigger sister, Vila Nova de Gaia has its own UNESCO World Heritage Site, Mosteiro da Serra do Pilar, a 16th-century monastery featuring a church and cloisters whose circular design is unique to Portugal. Revisiting Vila Nova de Gaia is the excuse to walk across the top deck of Dom Luís I Bridge and perhaps enjoy some port tasting – if you don't like port, the views back across the river are worth the journey.

Both the Coastal and Central Caminos depart from Porto at the cathedral, so even if you avoid cycling from there, you still have to visit. Construction began in the 12th century, and, perched atop the hill above the Ribeira district, its exterior retains Romanesque characteristics, particularly the towers overlooking the square on the west front. Inside, the Gothic cloister, featuring 18th-century azulejos, is the standout feature.

There is a lot of accommodation in Porto and in Vila Nova de Gaia on the south bank, including a huge quantity of room-only accommodation. To simplify the choice stick with places near the route, avoiding the busy, hilly

Street life in Porto

and complicated city centre. Suggestions in the App include accommodation all the way to Foz do Douro where the recommended route leaves Porto on the way north.

Finding somewhere to enjoy the views and have a pre-dinner drink is perhaps something all visitors to Porto aim for, so expect crowds. In addition to port tasting on the south bank, Mirrajazz, a very informal jazz venue on the north bank, has a roof-top bar which, if you're lucky with the crowds, fits the bill

Francesinha is not the only food on offer in Porto, and there are many places to eat including fine-dining venues like the Pedro Lemos, which is very close to the route and has a Michelin star. To combine a stroll with sightseeing and eating opportunities head to the primary market, the Bolhão, which has a good choice of venues including a vegetarian restaurant.

On the Sendero Litoral north of Viana do Castelo (Stage 2, Coastal Camino)

PORTO TO SANTIAGO DE COMPOSTELA

The Central Camino
The Coastal Camino
The Spiritual Variant
Link Route to Central Camino
Santiago de Compostela
Padrón
Pontevedra
Ourense
Vigo
Valença/Tui
A Guarda
Caminha
Viana do Castelo
Braga
Barcelos
Vila do Conde
Vila Real
Porto

INTRODUCTION

Lovely path north of Caldas de Reis (Stage 4, Central Camino from Porto to Santiago de Compostela)

There are two Caminos between Porto and Santiago de Compostela: the Central Camino (the continuation of the route from Lisbon), and the Coastal Camino. Technically, they are separate Caminos (the Portuguese Government didn't recognise the Coastal Camino until 2016), and both are very popular. Based on pilgrim arrivals in Santiago de Compostela, the Central Camino is the second most popular route, after the original and main route (the Camino Frances), with 19% of all arrivals, and the Coastal Camino is the third, with 15% of the total.

From Porto, the Camino is busy, and a trail of pilgrims often defines the route ahead. On the Central Camino, only 15% have walked from Lisbon with the rest starting their journey either at Porto or somewhere to the north, with Tui/Valença on the border particularly popular.

Although the Caminos are technically separate, cyclists should consider them together when planning a route. Switching between routes is straightforward, and finding a route that matches your cycling preferences and available time is likely to involve a combination of both.

From Porto, the Central Camino and the Coastal Camino start at the cathedral and follow a shared route heading north through the city and splitting just south of the airport. The Coastal Camino continues north-west, past the airport, then heads down to the coast to the south of Vila do Conde, whereas the Central Camino continues north to Arcos. For a first-time visitor, descending from the cathedral and cycling through Porto is really unpleasant, with no-entry signs and heavy traffic defining the route. To avoid this, the recommended route follows the coast out of the city up to Vila do Conde. Cyclists heading up the Central Camino then head inland to join the official route to Arcos. For completeness, the official routes for both Caminos are included in the app.

If your journey starts in Porto, chances are you will have arrived at the airport (Francisco Sá Carneiro Airport) located 10km to the north of the city. The best way into the city is to head west to the coast, join the recommended route, and then head south.

Porto rooftops

Porto streets

The cathedral in Porto

A wonderful bike mechanic in Porto

THE CENTRAL CAMINO

Cycling the Central Camino, it's possible to reach Santiago de Compostela in four days with overnight stops at Barcelos, Tui/Valença (on the border) and Pontevedra. The toughest day is Tui/Valença to Pontevedra, which includes a climb with off-road elements. The climb, however, can be easily avoided. The route follows a transport corridor north and occasionally traverses transport intersections, but most of it follows quiet roads interspersed with off-road tracks and paths.

The lovely bridge south of Arcos

Leaving Porto on the Sendero Litoral

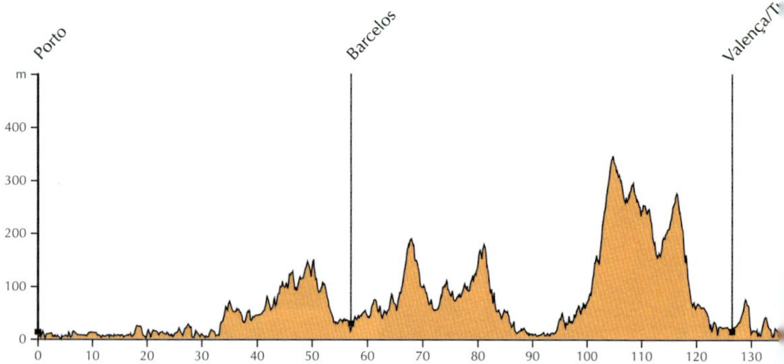

On the nature route north of Tui

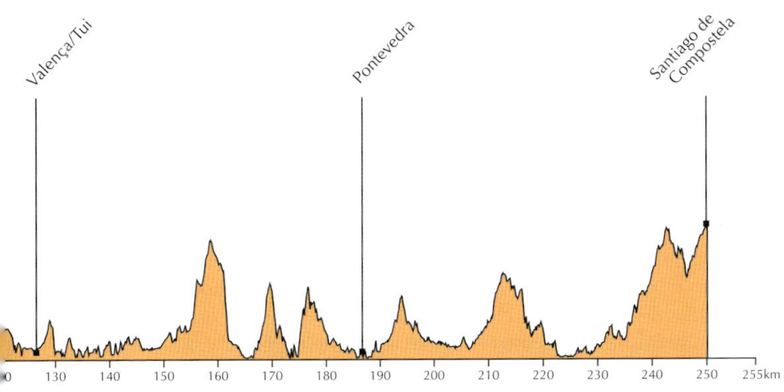

STAGE 1

Porto to Barcelos

Start	Porto
Finish	Barcelos
Time	5hr 15min
Distance	64km (39.8 miles)
Total ascent	463m
Total descent	412m
Terrain	Road (or cobbled) 49km, off-road 15km

Stage 1 assumes the recommended accommodation approach has been adopted and starts at Foz de Douro, near the mouth of the river. It heads north along the coast to Vila do Conde (which is the recommended Stage 1 stopover on the Coastal Camino) and heads inland to Barcelos, which is another 29km. The route crosses the River Ave at Vila do Conde and follows a cycle route to Arcos, where it joins the official Central Camino.

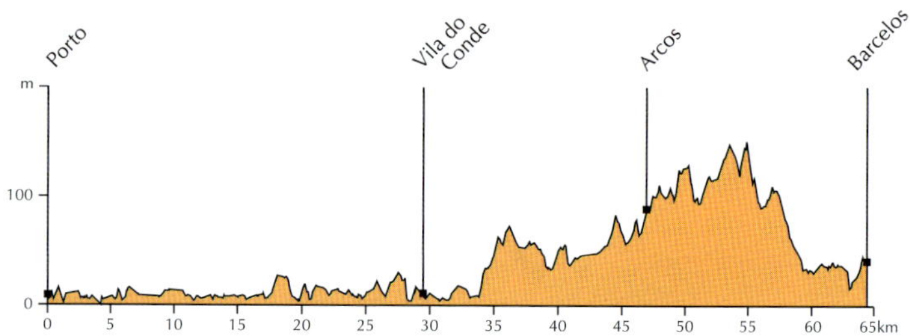

Porto to Vila do Conde 29.4km

Although the recommended route along the coast out of Porto is neither the official Coastal or the Central Camino, it is waymarked with Camino signs and used by pilgrims following the Coastal Camino. On the way to **Vila do Conde**, deviations from the waymarked route are needed to avoid one-way streets and wooden boardwalks where cycling is not allowed. Missing out on the boardwalks is especially frustrating, as they run right along the edge of the beach and look very attractive, which explains why pilgrims choose this route. Unfortunately, the

Vila do Conde
N
0
2
4
km
Castêlo da Maia
Route leaves boardwalk Camino
Lavra
Moreira
Maia
Perafita
Coastal Camino
Central Camino
Leça do Balio
Custóias
Route leaves boardwalk Camino
Guifões
Complex signage
Matosinhos
Senhora da Hora
Route avoids Camino one-way system
ATM
S
Porto

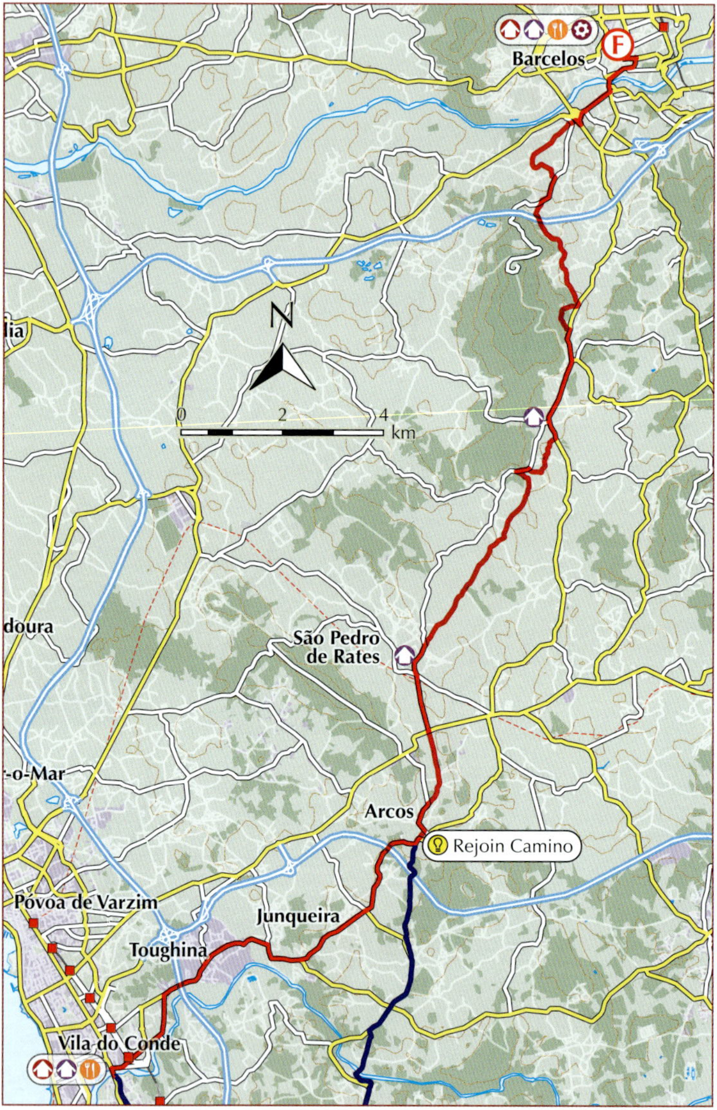
Barcelos
F
N
0
2
4
km
lia
doura
São Pedro
de Rates
-o-Mar
Arcos
Rejoin Camino
Póvoa de Varzim
Junqueira
Toughina
Vila do Conde

no-cycling signs are clear and frequent, and a negative response from locals is guaranteed if ignored. All the variations are minor, but there are many.

Apart from missing out on the boardwalks, cycling is easy and, with sea views, enjoyable. The main challenge is the roundabouts on either side of the bridge over the dock at Matosinhos. If in doubt, get off and use the footpath.

Vila do Conde to Barcelos 34.6km

There are no obvious waymarks between Vila do Conde and Arcos, but it's an easy road route (EN 309) to follow, and the little towns of Touginha and Junqueira are potential stopping points on the way. The route crosses the motorway and then joins the Camino, where, after crossing a lovely medieval bridge, it heads into **Arcos**. Just north of Arcos, it splits (for about 4km), with the recommended route following the easterly variant. There are now waymarks to follow all the way to **Barcelos**. After crossing the bridge on the way into Barcelos, there is a one-way system to avoid. The off-road cycling, some of which is hilly, starts at the 42km mark and continues for about 7km. It's a reasonably broad trail and not difficult.

The bridge at Barcelos

BARCELOS

Barcelos, designated a city, is located on the northern bank of the River Cávado, reached after crossing an impressive medieval bridge, and is famous for two things: the Rooster of Barcelos and the Barcelos market.

The rooster, actually a roasted rooster, saved the life of a Galician pilgrim who was being hanged for a crime he didn't commit – by crowing, the roasted rooster convinced the judge that the pilgrim was innocent. Although the rooster is associated with Barcelos and appears everywhere in the city, its fame is broader: an unofficial symbol of Portugal and a favoured subject for tattoo artists.

The market takes place every Thursday; it is the largest open-air market in Portugal, and one of the largest in Europe. It attracts huge crowds in the summer and seems to sell everything, including livestock. It is the very best place to buy a ceramic rooster.

The city's historic core is compact, and it's possible to visit all the main sites in a couple of hours. Recommended are the New Gate Tower, which houses a small museum, but closes quite early, and the nearby Baroque church. The medieval bridge, the church (the Igreja Matriz de Barcelos), and the Solar dos Pinheiros, a large house or small palace, form a sombre concentration of Gothic buildings. Finish your tour with a visit to Babette Wine & Tapas in a nearby square for a relaxing pre-dinner drink. For dinner consider the Turismo restaurant – really good food despite the name and the giant rooster near the door. There isn't a massive choice of hotels but for non-hostel accommodation, the Art'otel Barcelos, which has a small swimming pool, is very pleasant.

STAGE 2

Barcelos to Valença/Tui

Start	Barcelos
Finish	Valença/Tui
Time	6hr 15m
Distance	73km (45.4 miles)
Total ascent	1012m
Total descent	1008m
Terrain	50km road, 23km off-road

Stage 2 is by some margin the toughest of the whole route. Fortunately, there are options to match different cycling appetites.

The first option involves splitting the day in two and stopping at Ponte de Lima, a small but pretty town on the southern bank of the Rio Lima. Ponte de Lima is 33km from Barcelos.

The big climb, some 300m with steep off-road sections, occurs in the second half of the Stage, after Ponte de Lima, and a second, easier option follows a quiet, well-graded road up the pass.

There is also a make-it-harder option. The recommended route avoids a 4km off-road stretch of the Camino, often single-track, with an additional climb, and involves substantial bike carrying.

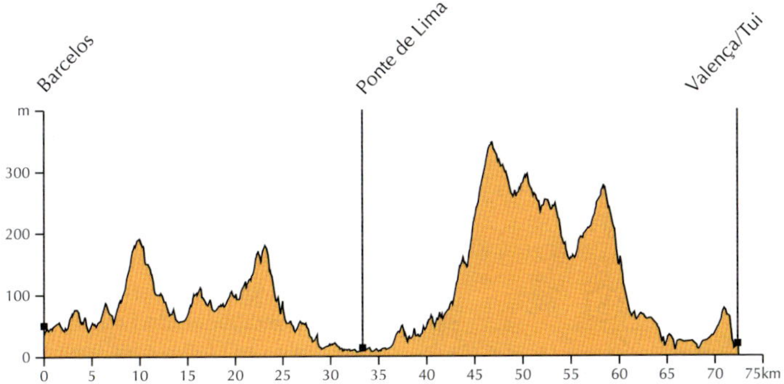

Barcelos to Ponte de Lima 33km

Waymarks can be followed all the way from Barcelos to **Ponte de Lima**, along quiet country roads with only the occasional short off-road stretch. If the weather is good, it's enjoyable cycling with just a couple of minor hills to contend with. For coffee, consider stopping at **Aborim**, at the Olivia café (where everyone is buying lottery tickets) or Rosa Cintilante, just a bit further on.

Ponte de Lima to Valença/Tui 40km

The decision on which route to follow to the pass, the recommended route or the road variant is marginal and depends on the weather and how wet the route is. If there has been heavy rain, then the first kilometre, crossing water meadows on the north side of the river, is likely to be waterlogged. The route follows a farm track to the village of **Arcozelo** before joining a single track for a section of the ugly cycling route beneath a motorway. It then starts to climb a steep, fortunately metalled, road before leaving the waymarks 12km after Ponte de Lima. If the weather is bad, the route is wet, and an easier day is preferred, take the road variant.

Continuing all the way over the pass on the Camino is not recommended, there are difficult sections involving a lot of bike carrying or pushing. The recommended route leaves the Camino and follows an empty road for 3km to the pass.

PONTE DE LIMA

Ponte de Lima is the oldest Portuguese town, the first to be granted a Royal Charter by the Portuguese monarchy, with its status derived from a stunning medieval bridge, built on Roman foundations, that crosses the River Lima. Most of the town's original fortifications have been dismantled, but the Tower Cadeia Velha, which houses the Tourist Information Office, indicates the scale of the town's original defences. In addition to its bridge and antiquity, Ponte de Lima is famous as the centre of the Vinho Verde wine district. If you have split the day into two, you will have time to visit the Paço do Marquês (Palace of the Marquis) located above the town, heavily restored but with Manueline windows and a nice garden.

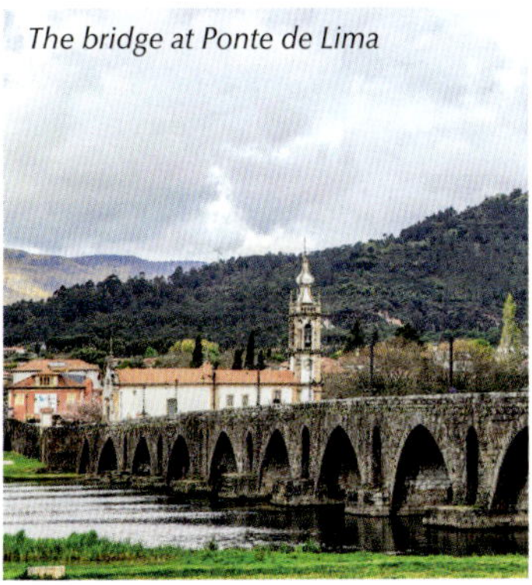

The bridge at Ponte de Lima

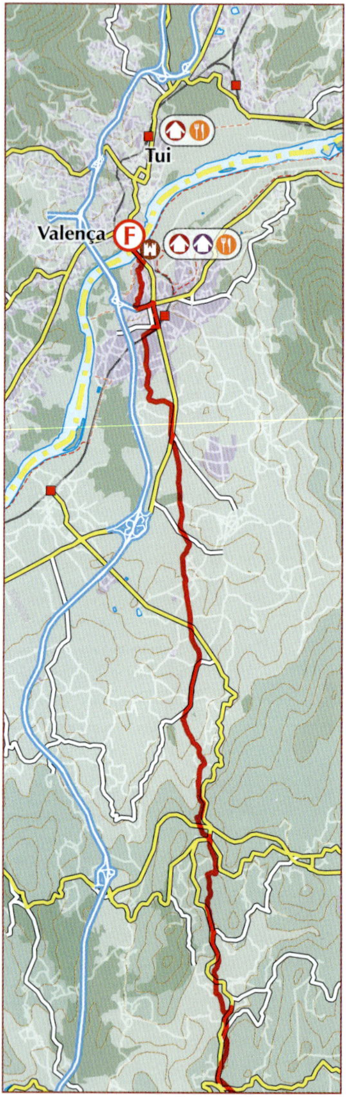

VALENÇA

Valença's most striking feature is its 17th-century fortress (the Fortaleza). Its walls, which are 5km long, form two polygons – the Praça and the Coroada – connected by a bridge. The best way to appreciate the fort's scale is to walk along the walls, but it will take about two hours. The walls enclose a small town with narrow cobbled streets and artisan shops specialising in lace, linen, and embroidery, and it is a magnet for Spanish tourists (particularly on market day, which is a Wednesday). The town is bustling during the day; it becomes strangely quiet once the tourists leave.

The recommended route and the road variant meet at the pass and descend for 3km before turning right onto a narrow lane to rejoin the Camino, which can then be followed all the way to **Valença/Tui**. The cycling is good, with a mix of quiet country roads and off-road tracks that cross from one side of the main road to the other. In poor weather, the attractions of the main road will be obvious.

TUI

Tui, just on the other side of the Minho River, feels different: less of a tourist destination and more like a lively Spanish town with a historic centre. Dominating the centre of the town is the cathedral, a huge, sombre granite edifice that combines Romanesque and Gothic styles and was built to serve both as a church and a fortress. The tower, which you can climb, provides great views of the river and Valença.

The wonderful bridge connecting Valença and Tui, with rail on the top deck and a road and pedestrian route on the deck below, was built to symbolise Spanish-Portuguese cooperation and was completed in the 1880s. Crossing it by bike is great fun.

Valença and Tui are two distinct destinations, and choosing where to stay is challenging. Both have a good choice of accommodation, including a parador in Tui and the equivalent Pousada in Valença. Having stayed in both towns, Tui was more fun in the evenings and, operating on Spanish time, provided a wider choice of food and drink venues with tapas bars around the square near the cathedral. Tui has a good choice of accommodation, including hostels with private rooms. If the parador is too expensive and a little out of the way, consider Lara (where I stayed on my second trip) or A Torre do Xudeu.

The International Bridge at Valença/Tui

The church of Santo Domingo in Tui

STAGE 3

Valença/Tui to Pontevedra

Start	Valença/Tui
Finish	Pontevedra
Time	4hr 50min
Distance	55.5km (34.5 miles)
Total ascent	654m
Total descent	656m
Terrain	42km road, 13.5km off-road

Things get noticeably busier on Stage 3, with many pilgrims starting their journey at Tui or even a bit further north to complete the minimum required hiking to qualify. As well as more pilgrims, the route itself is 'busy', visiting three towns en route (O Porriño, Redondela and A Ponte) and combining enjoyable off-road cycling with generally quiet country roads and some hills. The high-level train viaduct through Redondela is particularly spectacular, making it a great place to stop for lunch. With the Coastal Camino merging with the Central Camino, the sudden uptick in hikers is striking.

The Camino splits north of Tui and on the approach to O Porriño. The recommended route follows the more rural, westerly option (the 'nature route'), which involves more off-road cycling. It avoids the ugly cycling through an industrial estate and the one-way system in O Porriño.

Slight deviations from the Camino are needed to navigate the one-way system out of Tui, the one-way system in Redondela, and some really difficult and very crowded single track north of A Ponte. The route gets a little complicated in the middle of Pontevedra, but how tricky it is will depend on the choice of accommodation.

Valença/Tui to O Porriño 20km

If the weather has been dry and it's not raining, the cycling to **O Porriño** on the recommended route is excellent, mainly off-road, through trees with some lovely stretches along the side of a river and through a ford. If it's wet, route diversions may be in force. The split in the Camino kicks after this super pleasant wooded stretch.

The architect Antonio Palacios (1874–1945) was born in O Porriño and he designed many local buildings. His work often utilised pink granite (*Rosa Porriño*) from local quarries.

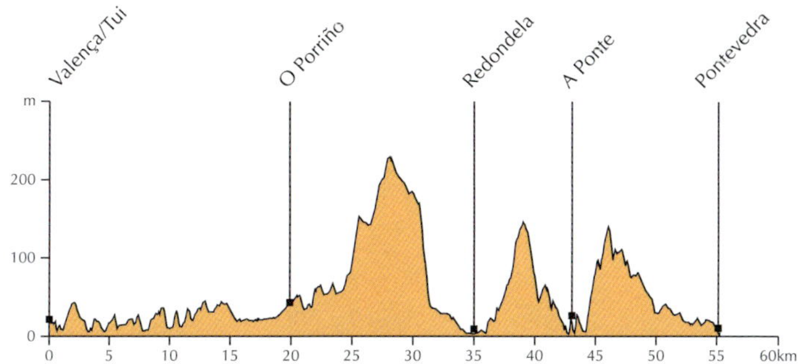

On the 'nature route' variant north of Tui

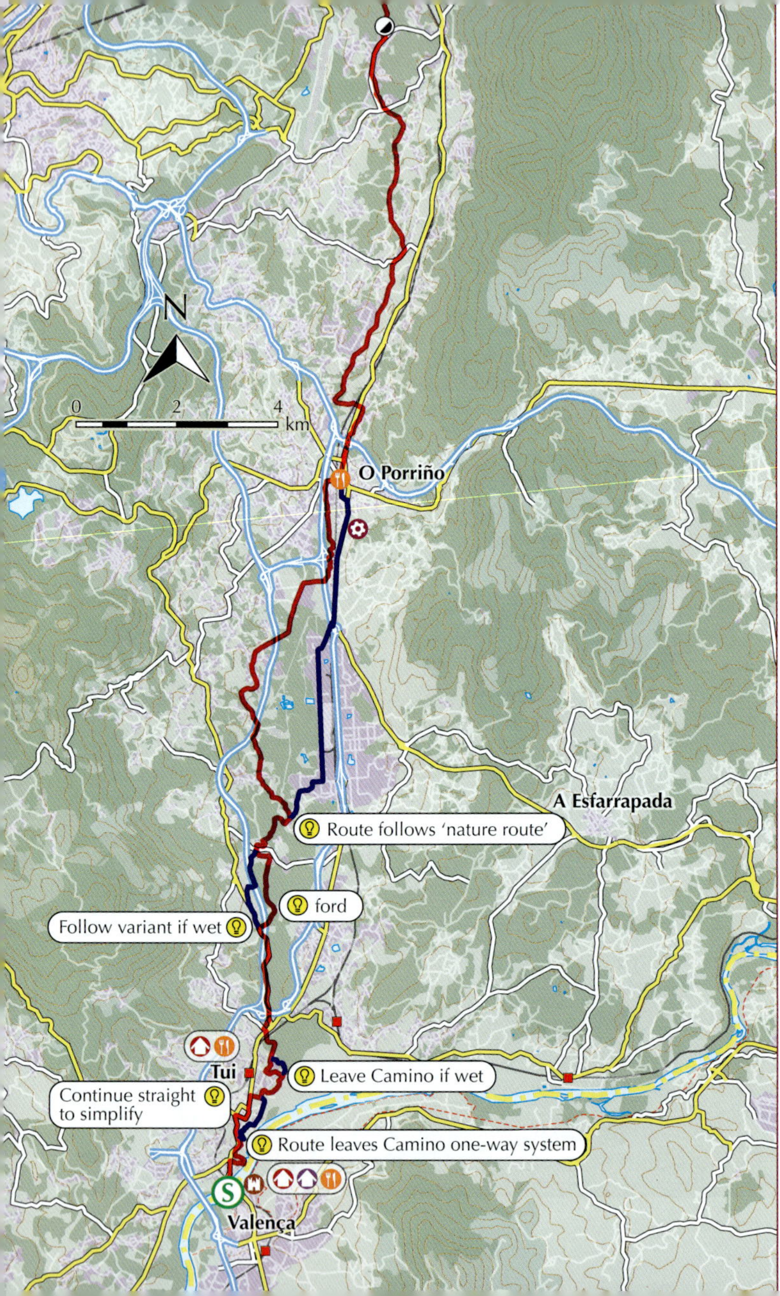
N
0
2
4
km
O Porriño
A Esfarrapada
Route follows 'nature route'
ford
Follow variant if wet
Tui
Leave Camino if wet
Continue straight to simplify
Route leaves Camino one-way system
Valença

REDONDELA

Redondela, set deep in a valley, is dominated by two viaducts. One, the Viaduct Pontevedra, still taking trains to Vigo, is 250m long and runs east to west high above the town; the other, the Viaduct Madrid, is 400m long, no longer used, and runs north-south to the east of the city. Redondela is a lovely town, full of pilgrims, of course, and with lots of places for refreshments.

Redondela to Pontevedra 20.5km

After the hustle and bustle of Redondela, the route embarks on another climb, about 100m on a quiet metalled road through trees, before descending to **A Ponte** crossing its lovely bridge. Leaving the Camino on the other side, it follows a nicely graded road up another hill, where, after a short stretch of off-road, it commences on a steady descent to **Pontevedra**.

100km to go and it gets busier

Resting up in Pontevedra

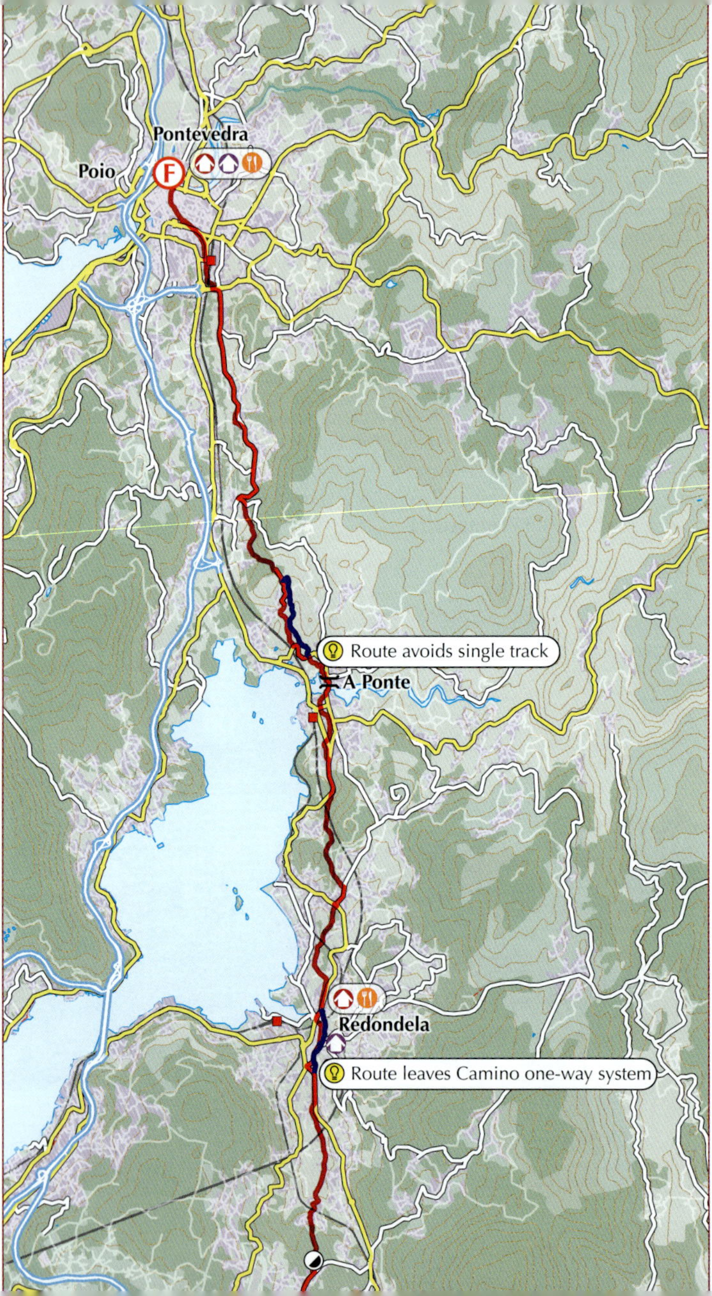
Pontevedra
Poio
F
Route avoids single track
A Ponte
Redondela
Route leaves Camino one-way system

PONTEVEDRA

Pontevedra is located at the mouth of the Lérez River, has a lovely pedestrianised historic core and, particularly at the weekend, but probably on other evenings, is a lively, even noisy place with great places to eat and drink.

In addition to visiting its restaurants, Pontevedra has two important churches. The Basilica of Saint Mary Major was built in the 16th century by the Sailors' Guild and is regarded as a Galician masterpiece that blends Gothic and Renaissance styles. Its Plateresque west façade resembles a stone altarpiece, featuring intricate carvings of biblical scenes and other figures, like Christopher Columbus. The statue of St Jerome on the main façade is notable because this fourth century theologian is wearing spectacles.

The Baroque Chapel of the Pilgrim Virgin reflects the city's association with the Camino, with the floorplan reflecting a scallop. Look out for the holy water font: a mollusc shell from the Pacific, acquired by Méndez Núñez, a 19th-century Spanish naval officer whose CV reads like that of an action hero.

Spain has its own version of Fatima in Pontevedra. The Sanctuary of the Apparitions, just north of the basilica, is the Catholic convent where Sister Lúcia, one of the three Fatima sisters, saw the child Jesus and the Virgin Mary in 1925–26, and is now the world's third-most-visited Marian pilgrimage destination.

Head to the medieval squares, such as Praza da Leña (Firewood Square) and Praza da Ferrería, and the nearby streets are great places to find food. The Praza da Leña is the more intimate of the two, with seating in the square, and it has a costly restaurant (Eirado, with a Michelin star) and two more typically priced options, along with a tapas bar. Pontevedra offers a range of accommodation but if sleep is a priority, be careful to avoid the places where people drink, they stay noisy for a long time. The parador in Pontevedra is good value and in a great location.

Some bits are best avoided

The Church of the Pilgrim Virgin in Pontevedra

STAGE 4

Pontevedra to Santiago de Compostela

Start	Pontevedra
Finish	Santiago de Compostela
Time	5hr 15min
Distance	64.5km (40 miles)
Total ascent	685m
Total descent	438m
Terrain	37.5km road, 27km off-road

Unless you're travelling on the Spiritual Variant, today is the last day on the Camino. Happily, apart from some very minor variations to avoid no-entry signs, you can follow Camino signs all the way to Santiago de Compostela. The cycling is good, with plenty of easy off-road along well-trodden agricultural roads, and just a bit of ugly cycling navigating the motorway interchange south of the destination. The route visits two significant towns, Caldas de Reis and Padrón, where a pepper stop is mandatory. If you have travelled all the way from Lisbon, reaching Santiago de Compostela will be a priority, and there is a lot to see and experience.

Pontevedra to Santiago de Compostela is a vital transport corridor, and with a new motorway and a modernised high-speed train route, it has benefitted from the renewal of Spain's transport infrastructure. This means that the old 'main' road, the N550, is now empty, and if you want to get to Santiago de Compostela early, it is the way to go.

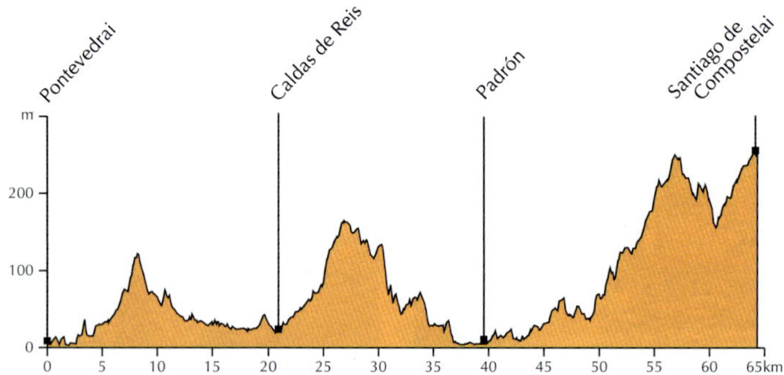

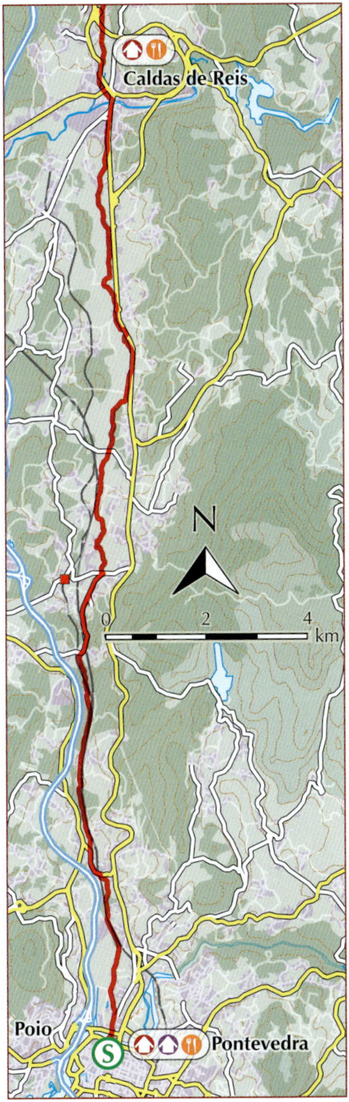

Pontevedra to Caldas de Reis 20.5km

After crossing the old bridge in Pontevedra and following a quiet, occasionally dirt road, close to a railway line, the route climbs around 100m through trees to a pass. Here it crosses a modernised stretch of the railway line before descending steadily down to **Caldas de Reis**.

Caldas de Reis is another important river crossing point (River Umia) featuring a lovely medieval bridge built on Roman foundations. It also features some thermal springs if needed.

Caldas de Reis to Padrón 18km

Another stretch of easy, mixed-surface cycling, a climb again through trees and a track that runs on one side of the motorway, crosses and then runs on the other before a long easy descent to **Padrón**, before crossing another medieval bridge built on Roman foundations at the entrance to the town.

Final day on the Camino – Capela de San Martin

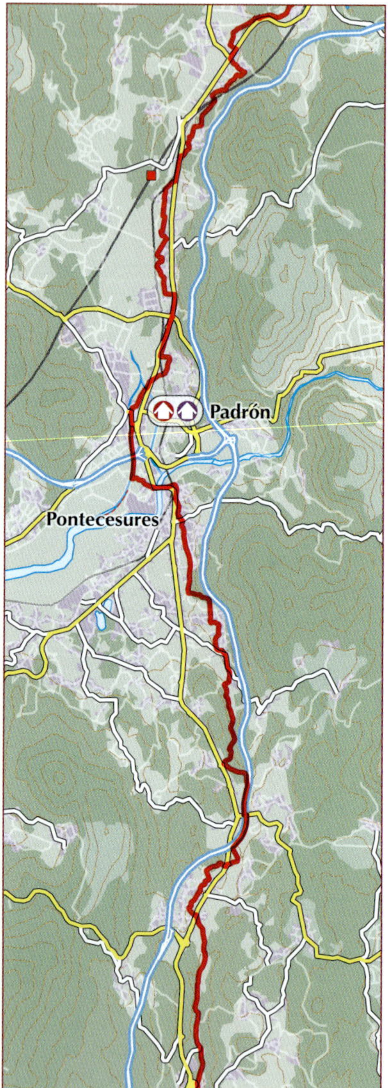

PADRÓN

Padrón is the last town before Santiago de Compostela and is supposed to be where the boat carrying the remains of St James the Apostle arrived in Spain. The Roman altar stone used to moor the boat is positioned under the altar in the Iglesia de Santiago Apóstol de Padrón, the town's main church. The town is famous for its peppers, fried in olive oil with a lot of salt, eaten throughout the world and consumed in great quantities at the August pepper festival. Eating the peppers is supposed to be, like life, a bit of a lottery, as instead of being mild and spicy about 10% are hot and fiery. As the Galician saying goes, *Os pementos de Padrón, uns pican e outros non,* which translates to: 'Like Padrón peppers, some are hot and others are not'.

If you can't make the festival, try to arrive on a Sunday and enjoy the market. It's one of the biggest in Galicia, has everything, but the main thing the huge crowds want is the *Pulpo a la Gallego* cooked in huge pans and consumed communally in vast tents on long tables.

The bridge into Padrón

Padrón to Santiago de Compostela 26km

The route is never far from the N550, crossing it several times, and then climbing steadily until it passes underneath a complex motorway junction, some hilly single track and a Roman bridge.

Fachada das Praterías – the cathedral in Santiago de Compostela

The ornate main altar in the cathedral in Santiago de Compostela

SANTIAGO DE COMPOSTELA

Santiago de Compostela is a remarkable place. Full of pilgrims descending on it from all directions, celebrating the end of their labours, underneath this perpetual invasion is a Galician city that works for its own inhabitants as well.

The city owes its pilgrimage origins to the discovery of the remains of St James there in the ninth century. By the tenth century, it was the third most important Christian destination after Rome and Jerusalem. What sets Santiago de Compostela apart, however, is the Camino. In 2023, over 440,000 pilgrims arrived in the city having completed at least 100km on one of the routes.

Gathering in the cathedral to watch the *Botafumeiro,* which smokes with incense and swings from its pulley, is the highlight of many pilgrims' visits to the city, and the cathedral is the heart of an impressive medieval centre. The current cathedral has a Romanesque core, but most of the façades were built later and are Baroque in character. On the western side is the magnificent Praza do Obradoiro, the main square of the old town and the place to get an end of trip picture. The northern part of the square is formed by the Hostal dos Reis Católicos, commissioned by Ferdinand and Isabella in 1499, now a parador and the oldest operating hotel in the world.

The medieval core of the city can be a very lively place, and in the narrow alleys to the north, locals mingle with pilgrims, keeping the bars and restaurants busy. The food in Santiago de Compostela is excellent, and the city has three Michelin-starred restaurants. For top quality tapas try Abastos 2.0 near the market, although my favourite restaurant, and good value, is the nearby Curro da Parra.

Souls in Purgatory

THE COASTAL CAMINO

The Coastal Camino to Santiago de Compostela, at 277.2km, is 20km longer than the Central Camino and, with stops at Vila do Conde, Viana do Castelo, A Guarda, Vigo and Pontevedra, takes two more days. Following the coastline (if you follow the recommended route), the Coastal Camino is longer but involves less ascent than the Central Camino.

The recommended route for Stage 1, to Vila do Conde, is the same for both the Central and Coastal Camino. It follows the Sendero Litoral. *Litoral* means 'coastal path' in both Spanish and Portuguese and is used on coastal paths around the Iberian peninsula. The Coastal Camino and Sendero Litoral are not always the same; from a cycling perspective, Sendero Litoral is often better and is recommended. The preference for a route that sticks to the coastline is shared by many walking pilgrims and, although it's not the official Coastal Camino, it is waymarked.

Instead of crossing into Spain over the River Minho on the ferry to A Guarda, there is a Camino that stays on the south side of the River and continues to Valença/Tui where it joins the Central Camino. This creates a five-day schedule to Santiago de Compostela and misses/avoids Vigo. This Coastal–Central Camino composite also means missing the biggest climb on the Central Camino.

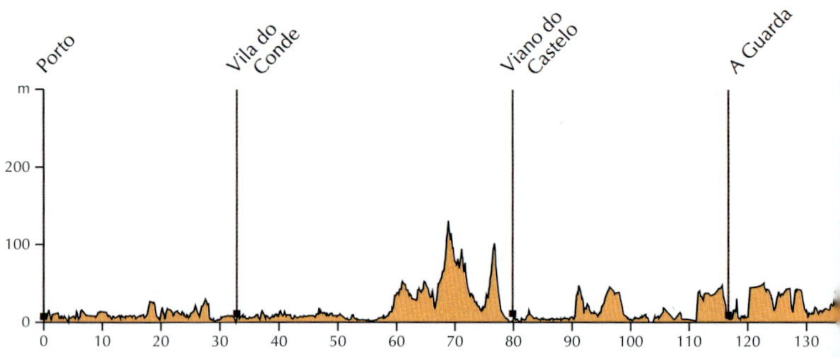

The rooftops of Vila do Conde (Stage 1, Coastal Camino)

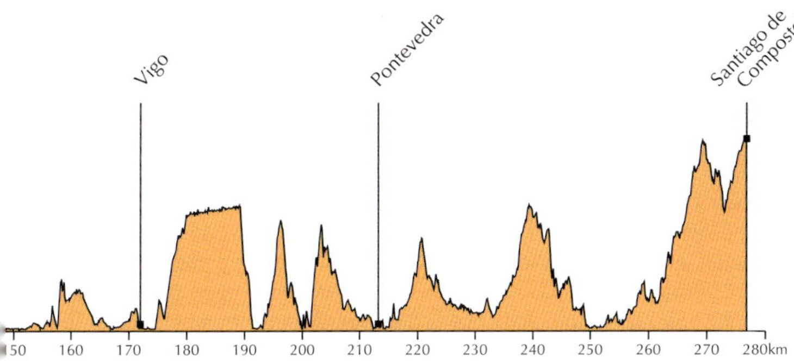

STAGE 1

Porto to Vila do Conde

Start	Porto
Finish	Vila do Conde
Time	2hr 10 min
Distance	29.4km (12.7 miles)
Total ascent	47m
Total descent	47m
Terrain	Road with cobbles

Stopping at Vila do Conde makes for a short and easy first day, but it makes sense because it's the best place to stop between Porto and Viana do Castelo, the must-visit Stage 2 destination.

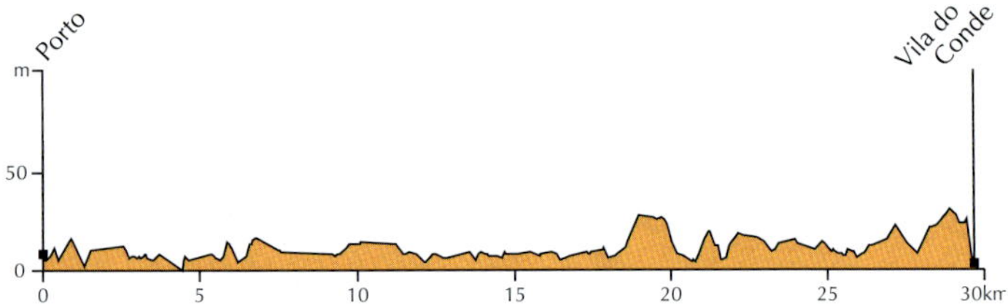

Porto to Vila do Conde

Although the recommended route along the coast out of Porto is neither the official Coastal or the Central Camino, it is waymarked with Camino signs and used by pilgrims following the Coastal Camino. On the way to **Vila do Conde**, deviations from the waymarked route are needed to avoid one-way streets and wooden boardwalks where cycling is not allowed. Missing out on the boardwalks is especially frustrating, as they run right along the edge of the beach and look very attractive, which explains why pilgrims choose this route. Unfortunately, the no-cycling signs are clear and frequent, and a negative response from locals is guaranteed if ignored. All the variations are minor, but there are many.

Apart from missing out on the boardwalks, cycling is easy and, with sea views, enjoyable. The main challenge is the roundabouts on either side of the bridge over the dock at Matosinhos. If in doubt, get off and use the footpath.

Tiled houses in Vila do Conde

VILA DO CONDE

With its brilliant hilltop location at the mouth of the River Avo, Vila do Conde is one of the oldest settlements in Portugal and was occupied well before the Romans arrived and built a fort and villas there. Following the Reconquest, the town became an important religious centre with the founding of the Monastery de Santa Clara in the 14th century. It then boomed during the Age of Discovery, becoming an important shipbuilding centre. Both legacies are evident today: the Monastery, now a five-star hotel, dominates the town from its hilltop location, and the *Nau Quinhentista*, a full-scale replica of a 16th-century Portuguese ship, is moored on the quayside near the bridge. Other important buildings include the Igreja Matriz church, which sits on one side of the town square, the Praça Vasco da Gama, and the Santa Clara aqueduct – built in the 17th and 18th centuries and the longest in Portugal.

Fridays host a particularly large market and, among many other things, features lace, the making of which is a local speciality, with Vila do Conde holding the Guinness World Record for the largest piece of bobbin lace.

The Praça da República, once a cattle market and the square to the left of the bridge facing the river, is the busiest square in the town with a line of restaurants offering al fresco dining. Two of the hotels on the app, the Naval Guest House and A Rendilheira Boutique Hotel are restaurants as well, enabling a very relaxed evening.

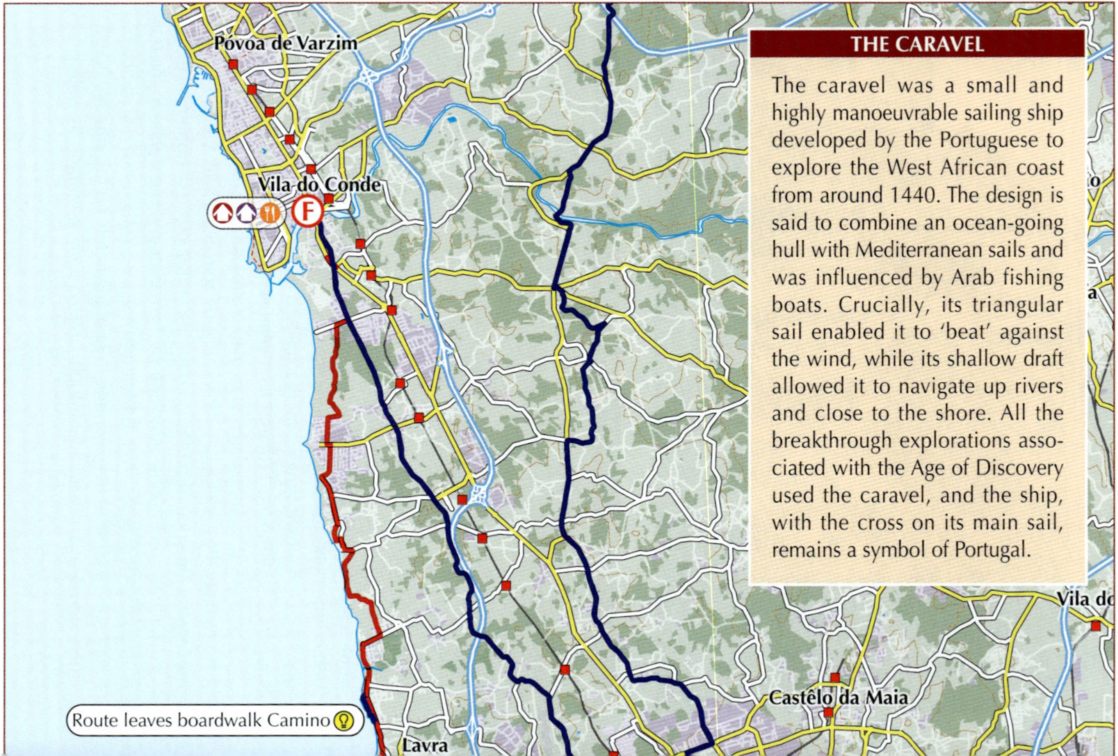

THE CARAVEL

The caravel was a small and highly manoeuvrable sailing ship developed by the Portuguese to explore the West African coast from around 1440. The design is said to combine an ocean-going hull with Mediterranean sails and was influenced by Arab fishing boats. Crucially, its triangular sail enabled it to 'beat' against the wind, while its shallow draft allowed it to navigate up rivers and close to the shore. All the breakthrough explorations associated with the Age of Discovery used the caravel, and the ship, with the cross on its main sail, remains a symbol of Portugal.

Maia
Leça do Balio
Custóias
São Mamede de Infesta
Senhora da Hora
Guifões
Matosinhos
Perafita
Porto
Vila Nova de Gaia
Route leaves boardwalk Camino
Complex signage
Route avoids Camino one-way system
N
0
2
4
km

STAGE 2

Vila do Conde to Viana do Castelo

Start	Vila do Conde
Finish	Viana do Castelo
Time	4hr
Distance	52km (32.3 miles)
Total ascent	270m
Total descent	263m
Terrain	39.5km road, 12.5km off-road

Ignoring the cobbles, Stage 2 is an easy day, basically flat but with a hilly sting in the tail. Excluding deviations for no-entry signs on one-way streets and no-cycling signs on boardwalks, it is possible to navigate using the waymarks. There is one stretch where the recommended route deviates to avoid carrying the bike. Still, it's on a lovely scenic route, and it might be worth the hardship to experience the view. In addition, there are a couple of potential variations to avoid off-road or harder cycling.

There are many places along the route for coffee and other refreshments but Esposende, which is halfway, is a logical breakpoint.

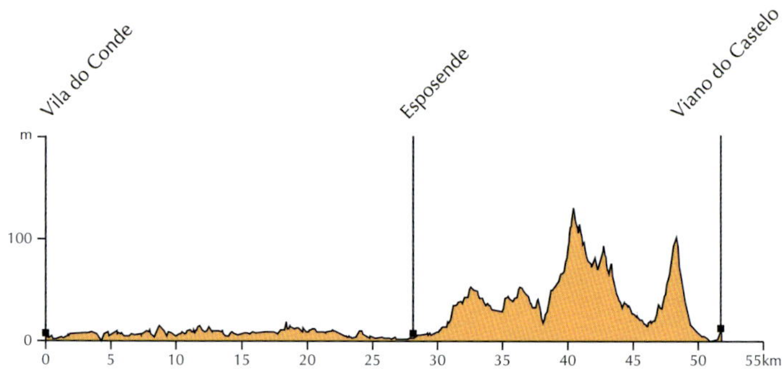

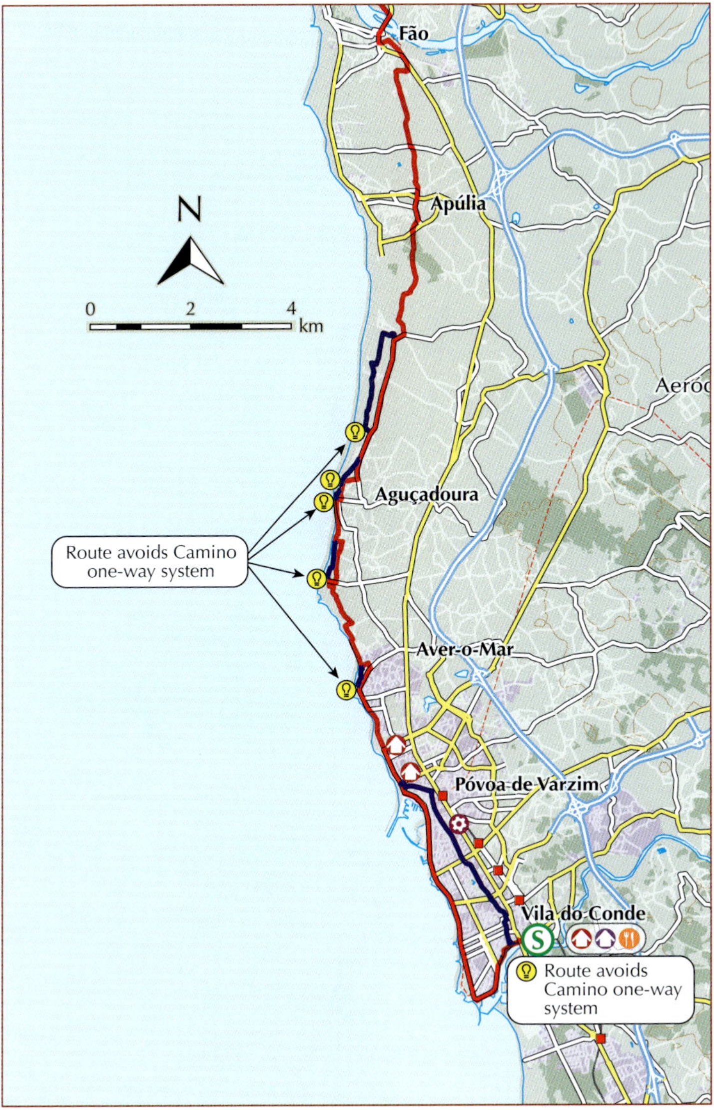
Fão
Apúlia
N
0
2
4
km
Aeróc
Aguçadoura
Route avoids Camino one-way system
Aver-o-Mar
Póvoa-de-Varzim
Vila do Conde
S
Route avoids Camino one-way system

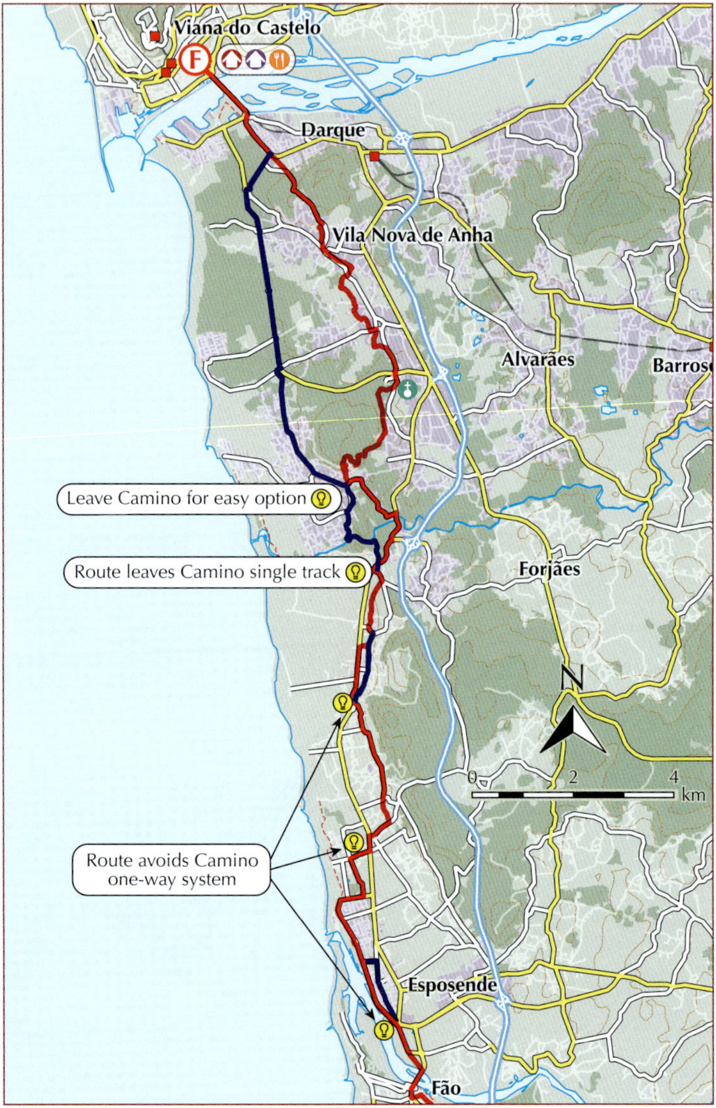
Viana do Castelo
F
Darque
Vila Nova de Anha
Alvarães
Barros
Leave Camino for easy option
Route leaves Camino single track
Forjães
N
0
2
4
km
Route avoids Camino one-way system
Esposende
Fão

Vila do Conde to Esposende 27.5km

Instead of the one-way streets and cobbles in the centre of Vila do Conde, the recommended route takes a more scenic route and rejoins the Camino at the little port of **Póvoa de Varzim**. North of the town, there are boardwalk diversions and, with the alternative often a cobbled road, cyclists feel like second-class pilgrims. The route follows the coast until **Apúlia**, where the Camino turns inland along sandy off-road tracks. For a potentially more scenic and easier route, consider following the coastal road along EuroVelo 1 for 5.2km, then rejoining the Camino at the bridge in Fão. The recommended route then stays on the coastal road to avoid the one-way system in **Esposende**.

Esposende to Viana do Castelo 24.5km

Following the Camino inland, there are a couple of one-way systems at Marinhas and Belinho, where the recommended route follows the 'main' road (which is still quiet). At 37km, the Camino descends to the river, turns west, and follows a single track through the trees, eventually crossing the river on stepping stones. It's a beautiful spot which the recommended route misses, and it also misses the steep climb on the other side of the river

The recommended route rejoins the Camino just before it begins its climb up to Igreja de Santiago de Castelo de Neiva, after which there is a sustained stretch of off-road cycling through trees and another climb. The recommended route turns right onto the Camino, but to avoid the climb, stay on the road (the EN13-3) and follow it to **Viana do Castelo**.

Lost in the flowers

VIANA DO CASTELO

Viana do Castelo is another beautifully located ancient city that blossomed as the most important port during the Age of Discovery. Its shipyards built the caravels that enabled explorers to trade with Brazil and Africa, financing its development. The most iconic architecture, Manueline and Renaissance, is found at the main square, the Praça da República, with its Renaissance fountain, fortress-like old Town Hall and the Misericórdia Hospital. The square has lots of lovely cafés and is the place to sit and relax.

Dominating the skyline and hard to access other than by the funicular railway is the 20th-century Santa Luzia basilica, a wedding-cake building with more than a passing resemblance to the Sacré-Cœur in Paris. The views from the top, particularly if you climb the tower, of the city and down the coast are amazing.

Viana do Castelo is where the Portuguese national dish, *bacalhau*, first entered the country, and the city has its own version (cooked in cabbage leaves). Its connections with cod can be explored at the Gil Eannes hospital ship. The ship, built in Viana do Castelo in 1955 to support the Portuguese cod-fishing fleet operating near Newfoundland and Greenland, has been restored and is open to the public.

In addition to bacalhau, the origin of the Portuguese national costume – the distinct red Lavradeira – has been bagged by Viana do Castelo. Not holding back, the claim is celebrated every August at the festival Romaria de Nossa Senhora d'Agonia, when hundreds of women (*mordomas*) parade through the streets wearing traditional costumes and kilos of intricate filigree gold jewellery. The festival is, of course, promoted as the world's largest open-air gold display!

The multi-level bridge on the way into the city, the Ponte Eiffel, was designed by Gustave Eiffel, best known for the Eiffel Tower.

Viana do Castelo has plenty of accommodation. The pousada looks amazing, with wonderful views down the coast, but is a bit out of the way. Better situated, and a wonderful hotel, is the Hotel Jardim Viana where you eat breakfast accompanied by a pianist. The Praça da República is the place for a pre-dinner drink, and in the square, and the narrow streets between the square and the river, there are lots of places to eat. Included is 360° by hygge&healthy, a health food restaurant. To celebrate the home of bacalhau, head down to the docks and enjoy fish at the Tasquinha da Linda.

Murals in Viana do Castelo

Santa Luzia Basilica – Viana do Castelo

Outside the Hotel Jardim Viana

STAGE 3

Viana do Castelo to A Guarda

Start	Viana do Castelo
Finish	A Guarda
Time	2hr 40min
Distance	36.5km (22.7 miles)
Total ascent	150m
Total descent	144m
Terrain	22km road, 14.5km off-road

Stage 3 and the Coastal Camino crosses the border by ferry into Spain – no more cobbles! Stage 3 also includes the option of staying in Portugal and heading east along the south bank of the River Minho and crossing into Spain at Tui. Depending on the route chosen, the Camino or the cycle track, this adds another 23km but avoids the ferry. It takes about two hours from Caminha.

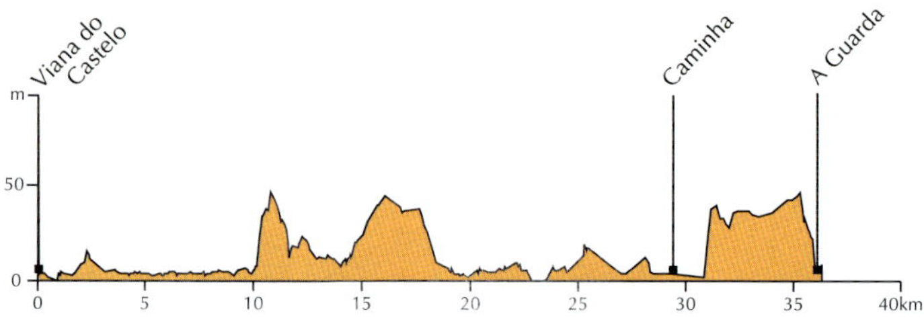

Viana do Castelo to Caminha 29.5km

From Viana do Castelo, the official Central Camino follows an inland route parallel to the coast, with a mixed-surface route that includes short, unpleasant stretches often wet with streams running down from the nearby hills. From a cycling perspective, it's not pleasant and the recommended route follows the Sendero Litoral, a lovely route running close to the coast. The Sendero Litoral joins the Coastal Camino at **Vila Praia de Âncora** and follows it to **Caminha**. The main street in Caminha is one-way and runs the wrong way, so to get to the ferry, the recommended route is to stay on the riverside road.

A Guarda
F
Route leaves Camino to avoid single track
Caminha
N
0
2
4
km
Vila Praia de Âncora
Viana do Castelo
S
Route follows Sendero Litoral
Darque

Crossing the River Minho

THE FERRY

There used to be a car ferry, but it has now gone, and local fishermen transfer passengers across the River Minho on a first-come, first-served basis. The small boats took four bikes on my journey, which didn't cause a problem. Expect to pay around ten euros, and remember the clocks change as you cross to the other side.

Caminha to A Guarda **7km (includes ferry)**

The Coastal Camino takes a direct route to **A Guarda** located on the western side of the hilly peninsula. It's a challenging route with some difficult single tracks. The recommended route follows a scenic coastal path around the peninsula on a lovely cobble-free road (no cobbles in Spain).

CAMINHA

If you follow the recommended route and you're in a rush to catch the ferry, chances are you'll miss out on the impressive town centre that reflects its wealthy past. At its heart is a medieval main square, the Praça Conselheiro Silva Torres, centred around a 16th-century Renaissance fountain. The clock tower, the Torre do Relógio, a former defensive gate, dominates the skyline with the main church, the Igreja Matriz de Caminha, at the other end of the main street, completing the impressive portfolio of Gothic and Manueline buildings.

A GUARDA

A Guarda is a pretty seaside town with a lovely harbour lined with restaurants. It's famous for its seafood, particularly lobster, which is celebrated at the annual Festa da Langosta in early July. Look out for the Indianos, colourful houses with ceramic tiles and wrought-iron balconies, built in the second half of the 19th and early 20th centuries by A Guarda emigrants to Puerto Rico, the Dominican Republic, and Brazil.

If the weather is good and you have plenty of energy, a walk up to the hill at Monte Santa Trega to visit the Bronze Age, Celtic hill fort, the associated museum, and to enjoy the views is well worth it.

Hotel Convento de San Benito, in a historic building, the best hotel in A Guarda and will be busy with pilgrims. There is a huge choice of harbour-facing restaurants offering similar fish feasts.

Hotel Convento de San Benito in A Guarda

LINK ROUTE TO CENTRAL CAMINO

Caminha to Valença/Tui

Start	Caminha
Finish	Valença/Tui
Time	2hr 10min
Distance	30.5km (19 miles)
Total ascent	350m
Total descent	330m
Terrain	Metalled 24km, 6.5km off-road

There are two ways to get from Caminha to Valença/Tui: on the Camino (the waymarked route), or on the Ecopista do Rio Minho, a cycle route. Apart from the fact that the cycle route follows the river, mainly on a purpose-built cycle trail with lovely views, there is no reason not to do the Camino.

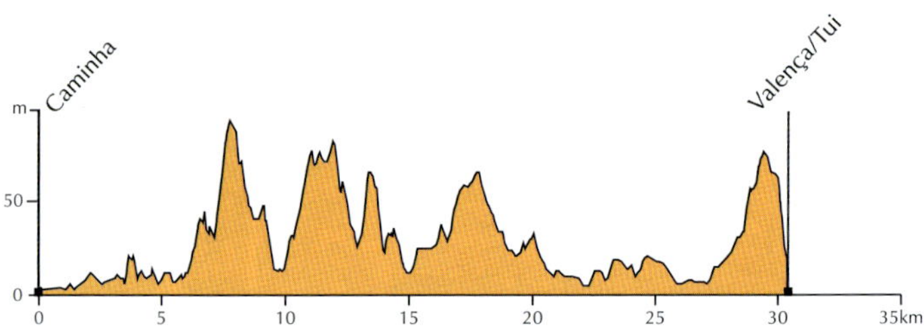

Caminha to Valença/Tui 30.5km

The Camino route is inland, slightly longer than the Ecopista do Rio Minho, involves more climbing and, apart from a hill on a track near where the route crosses over the motorway, the cycling is not challenging. It's a tough choice – the cycle trail is easier and prettier, and arrives at the same place, but it's not the Camino.

The medieval gate tower in Caminha

O Rosal
A Guarda
Sendero Litoral
or Camino
Caminha

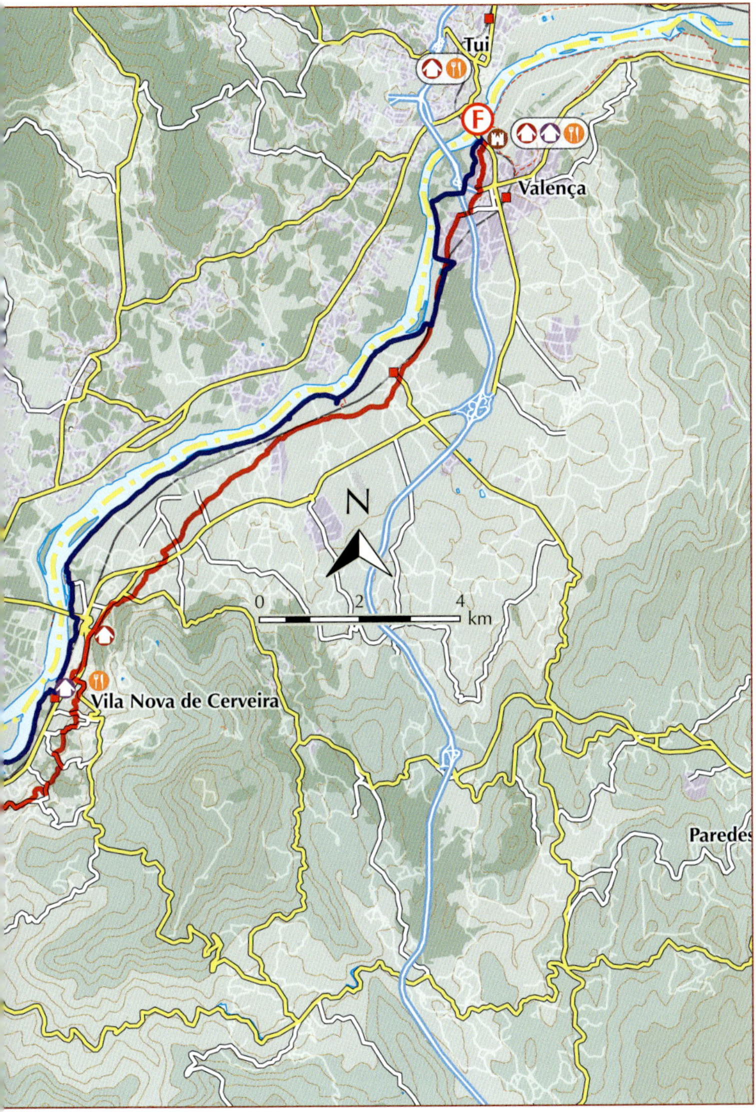
Tui
F
Valença
N
0
2
4
km
Vila Nova de Cerveira
Paredes

STAGE 4

A Guarda to Vigo

Start	A Guarda
Finish	Vigo
Time	5hr
Distance	58km (36 miles)
Total ascent	395m
Total descent	333m
Terrain	40km road, 18km off-road

The cycling, north up the coast and round to Baiona, is excellent and, apart from some minor variations, follows the Camino. After crossing the bridge at A Ramallosa, the Coastal Camino heads inland on a route that involves some challenging cycling. There are variants, with the Camino splitting, and even with the waymarks, the route is difficult to follow. Although the forest tracks are attractive, there are also some ugly bits as the route navigates its way past the Stellantis car factory. Finally, if that's not enough to put you off, the Camino doesn't actually go into Vigo, and you have to leave it to get to the city centre. The alternative and recommended route follows the Litoral route as far as possible, although boardwalks and one-way streets make this a little challenging at times.

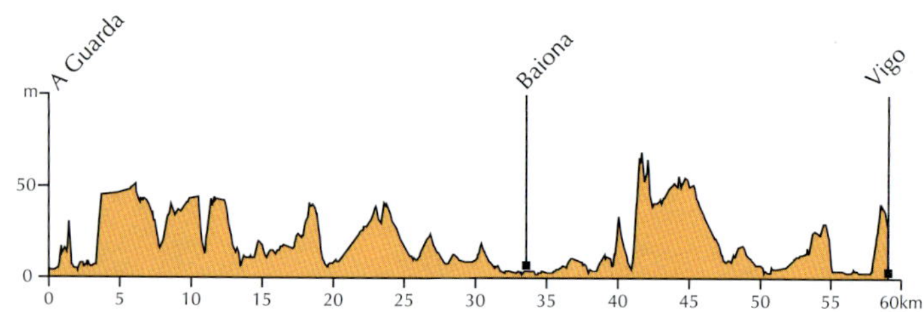

Route leaves Camino, single track
N
0
2
4
km
O Rosal
Route leaves Camino, single track
A Guarda
S

A Guarda to Baiona 33km

The recommended route grabs the last bit of the views and stays with the road around the harbour at A Guarda before joining the Camino on a track that runs on top of low cliffs. It then joins the main road, which runs all the way to **Baiona**, with Camino following it, leaving it on one side and then the other. The recommended route follows the Camino but avoids a couple of short descents at the northern end of the peninsula and doesn't follow the Camino on single track over the hill.

The Hotel Faro Silleiro is a hotel and restaurant in a working lighthouse, located at a right angle along the coastline. It's expensive, but in a special location and there is a café if you can't afford to stay.

Baiona to Vigo 25km

The Litoral is waymarked, but to avoid one-way streets and some boardwalks, there are many deviations. If the navigation becomes frustrating, the alternative is to stay on a reasonably quiet main road. Incidentally, the Vigo council has plans for a cycleway, the Gran Carril Litoral, running the full length of the city's seafront, but as yet these haven't been fully realised.

On the cycle track north of A Guarda

BAIONA

Originally a Celtic settlement, Baiona was the main commercial centre until Vigo developed in the 19th century. It was the first place to hear that Columbus had reached America when *La Pinta* arrived here in 1493, and this event is celebrated annually in the August Arribada (arrival) festival. The most distinctive building is the Monterreal Fort, which features a splendid tower and three miles of defensive walls. The fort is now a Parador and makes the town an alternative stopover if you don't fancy Vigo.

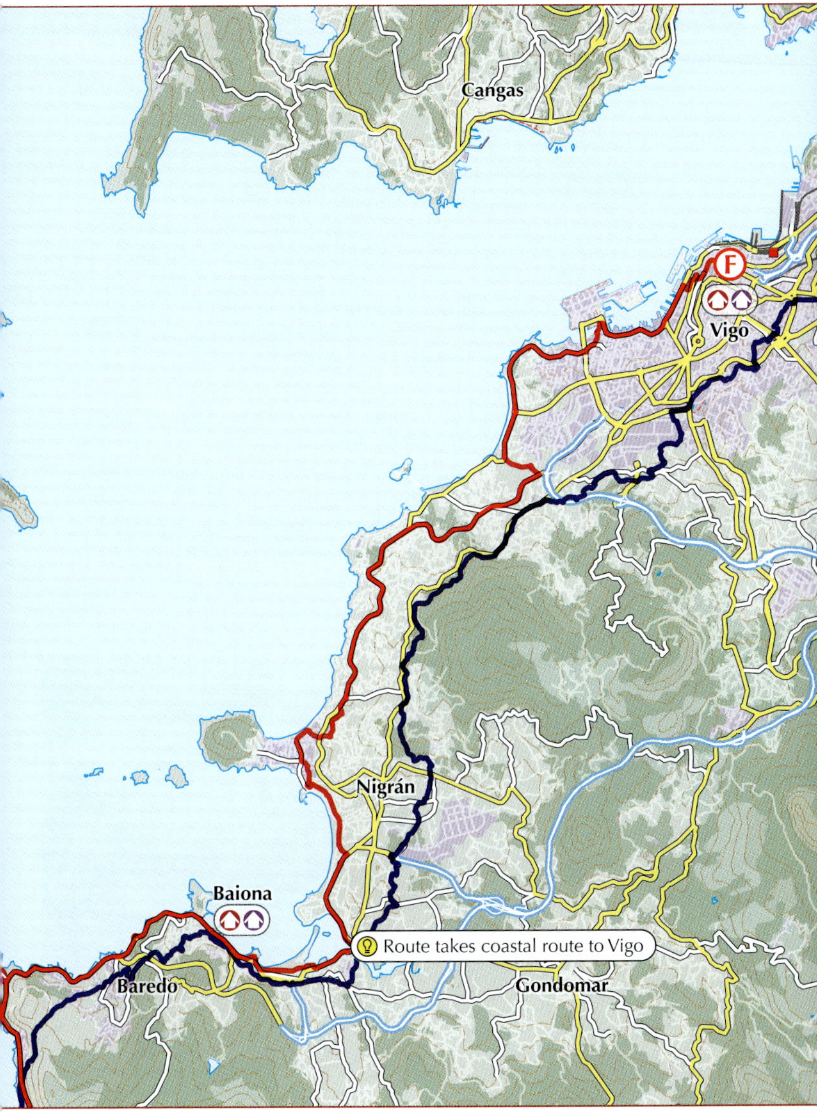
Cangas
F
Vigo
Nigrán
Baiona
Route takes coastal route to Vigo
Baredo
Gondomar

VIGO

Vigo has a Celtic, Roman, and Medieval past, but its current size and significance are a more recent development, dating in particular to the 1940s, when it was designated a freeport. The city is home to a major car plant and is the biggest fishing port in Europe; its fishing industry is associated with a large food-processing and canning industry.

The city sits on the southern banks of the Vigo Estuary, and just inland from its docks is a steep hill. This excellent defensive position has been fortified by successive occupants dating back to the Celts. On top of the hill, surrounding the ruins of the fortifications, the Fortaleza do Castro, is a park with great views across the estuary to the north.

From a visitor's point of view, the most interesting part of the city is the Casco Vello (the Old Town) located between the hill and the docks. It's a nice place for a stroll, and with its narrow streets and squares, the architecture feels older than the 19th century. There are lots of places to eat in Casco Vello, but make sure you visit the Mercado da Pedra, open all week and very crowded on weekends. The market is an essential gastronomic destination that sells all sorts of food, but is particularly famous for its seafood, especially oysters, which arrive each day from the nearby beds on the Cíes Islands. The oysters are available for immediate consumption and are typically served with a glass of local Albariño.

Street furniture in Vigo

STAGE 5

Vigo to Pontevedra

Start	Vigo
Finish	Pontevedra
Time	4hr 15 min
Distance	36.8km (22.9 miles)
Total ascent	476m
Total descent	511m
Terrain	26.1km road, 10.7km off-road

A short final stage on the Coastal Camino into the charming town of Redondela, known for its two 19th-century viaducts. Redondela is where the route joins the Central Camino and continues to Pontevedra.

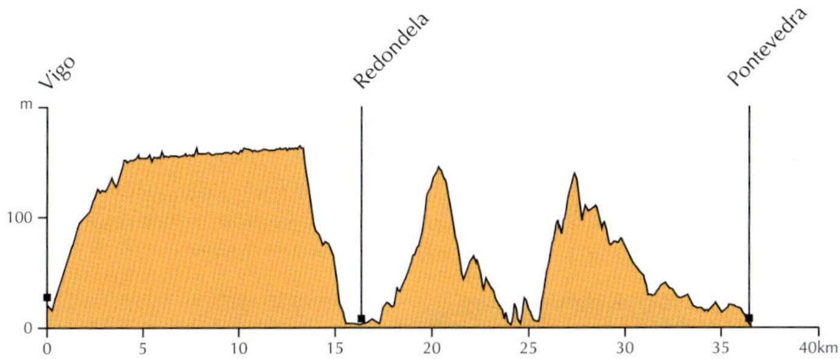

Vigo to Redondela 16.3km

Heading southeast from the centre of Vigo, the recommended route joins the Camino after 2km. Climbing gently out of the city on a road that gets quieter and more rural, the route eventually joins a flat forest track. The cycling is excellent, with great views of the elegant suspension bridge in the valley to the north. At 13km, the route descends steeply to **Redondela**.

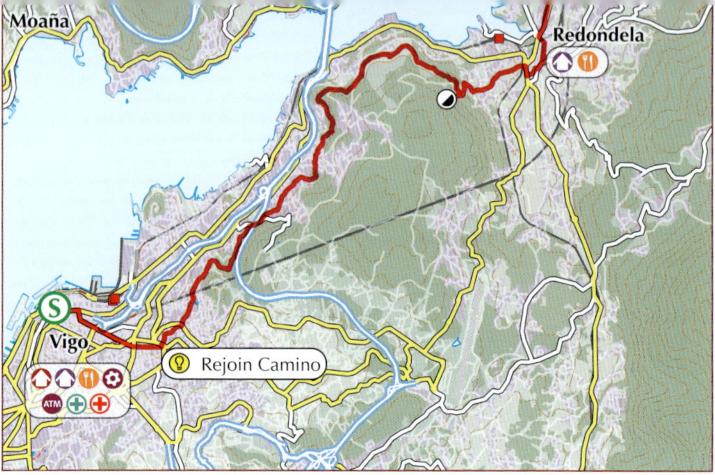

Redondela to Pontevedra 20.5km

At Redondela the route joins the Central Camino. After Redondela, the route climbs about 100m on a quiet metalled road through trees, before descending to **A Ponte**, crossing its lovely bridge. Leaving the Camino on the other side, to avoid a difficult stretch of crowded single track, the recommended route follows a nicely graded road up another hill, where – after a short stretch of off-road – it commences on a steady descent to **Pontevedra**.

From Pontevedra, either carry on to Santiago de Compostela (see Stage 4 of the Central Camino) or take the Spiritual Variant to Padrón before rejoining the Central Camino for the final leg of your Camino cycling adventure.

The elegant Rande Bridge (Puente de Rande)

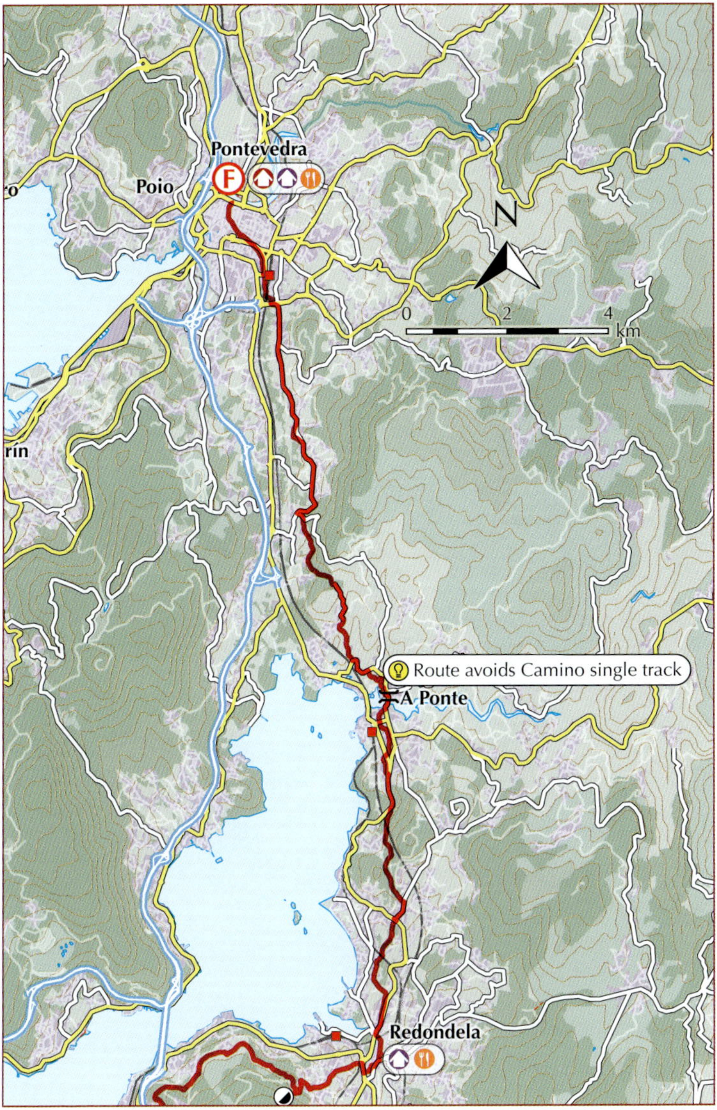
Pontevedra
F
Poio
N
0
2
4
km
Route avoids Camino single track
A Ponte
Redondela

Through the forest to the east of Vigo

Early morning at Combarro

THE SPIRITUAL VARIANT

From Pontevedra, the Spiritual Variant heads west along the southern coast of a peninsula, climbs over it and then heads east along its northern coast to Padrón. Although the Spiritual Variant features the route's most challenging climb, it requires only a single day of cycling. If 78km and a climb are too much, there are plenty of places to stay on the route, or you could reduce the journey to 46km by catching a ferry. The Traslatio makes the same journey as the boat carrying St James' body in AD44.

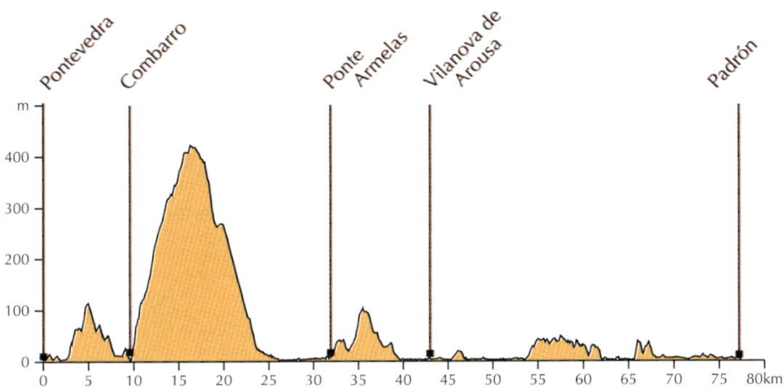

STAGE 1

Pontevedra to Padrón

Start	Pontevedra
Finish	Padrón
Time	7hr
Distance	78.2km (48.6 miles)
Ascent	850m
Descent	850m
Terrain	53km road, 25.2km off-road

The Spiritual Variant is a contender for the best day's cycling on the whole route. Please include it if you have time. It is a long day, but all the hard work is completed early on, and after cycling over the peninsula, the ride along the coast to Padrón is flat and easy. If it's too far, split the day into two and stay at Vilanova de Arousa or Cambados. You can also catch a ferry from Vilanova de Arousa and emulate St James (see below – the Traslatio).

Pontevedra to Combarro 10.2km

Getting to Combarro, a pretty seaside town facing east, is the day's biggest navigational challenge and a combination of one-way roads and some awkward single track means the recommended route ignores the waymarks and follows a non-Camino route for much of the first 10km.

Combarro to Ponte Armelas 22km

The climb from Combarro to the top of the hill is 420m, the most significant single climb on the whole route. Fortunately, most of it is on a metalled road and not too steep, with the final bit off-road but on a wide, non-challenging forest track. The first deviation from the Camino is on the other side of the hill. It avoids some steep single track as the Camino takes a direct route down to the monastery, Mosteiro de Santa María da Armenteira.

Watermills

Approaching Padrón

Waterfront at Vilanova de Arousa

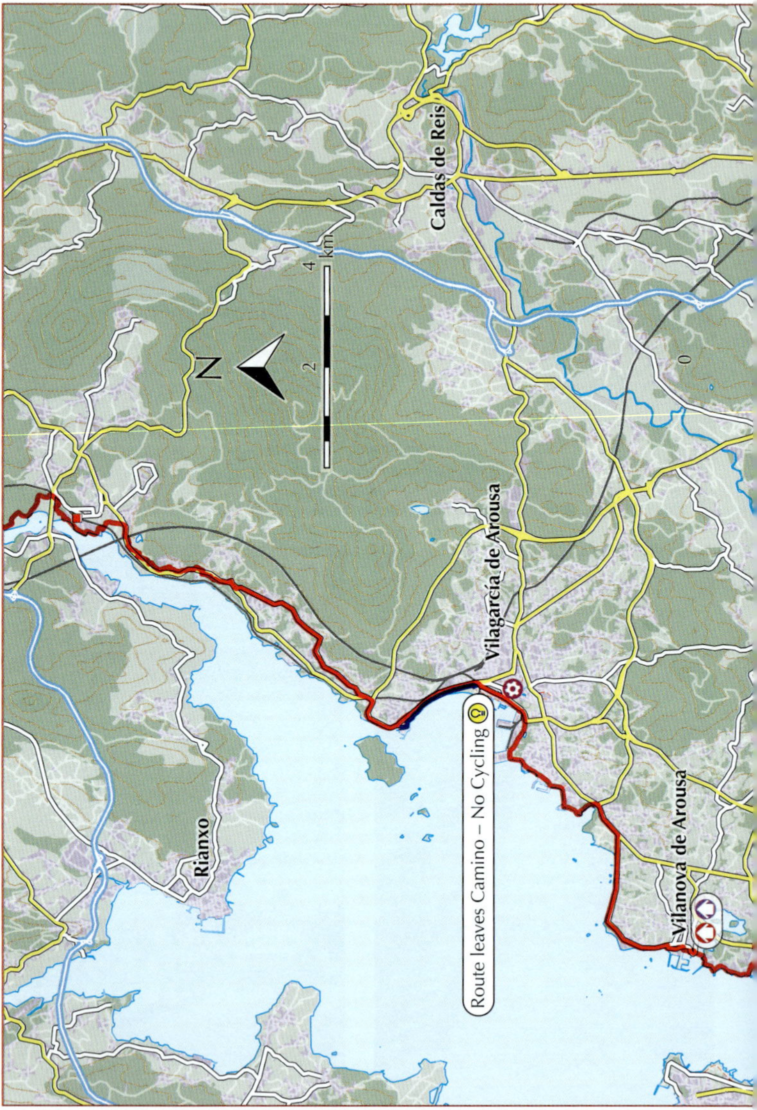
Caldas de Reis
Vilagarcía de Arousa
Rianxo
Vilanova de Arousa
Route leaves Camino – No Cycling
N
0
2
4 km

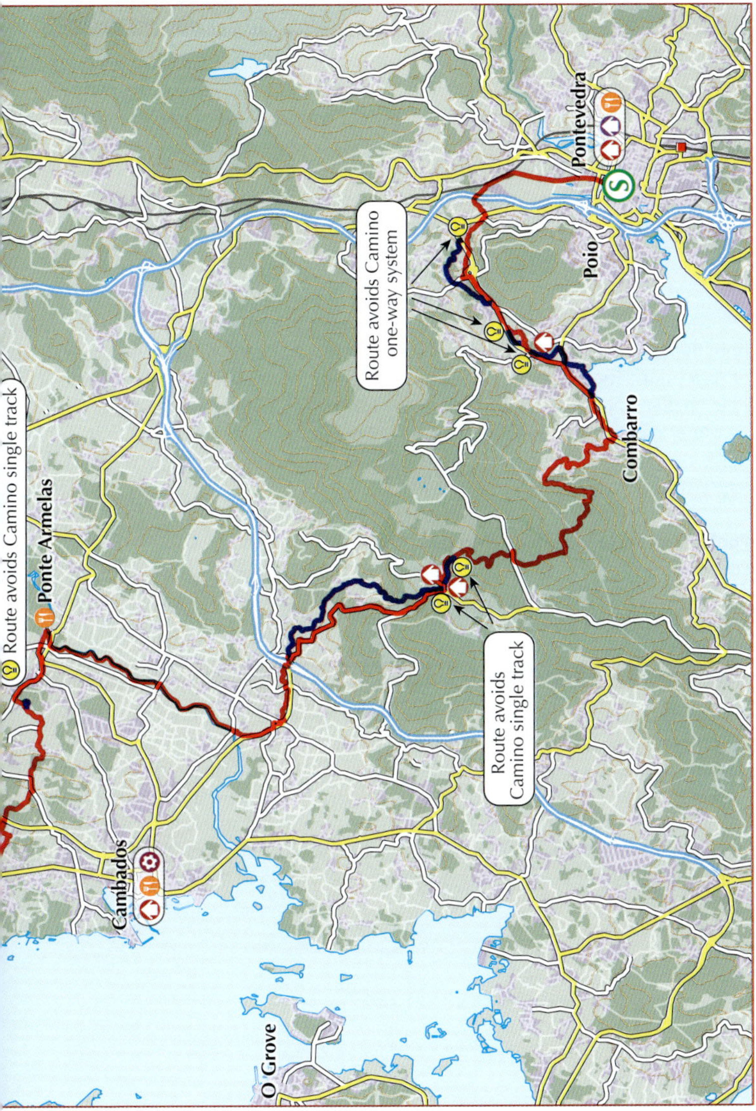
Pontevedra
Poio
Route avoids Camino one-way system
Combarro
Route avoids Camino single track
Route avoids Camino single track
Ponte Armelas
Cambados
O Grove

VILANOVA DE AROUSA OR CAMBADOS?

If you have enough time, consider splitting the Spiritual Variant into two. Vilanova de Arousa is the obvious place on the route but Cambados, a town just to the south, is much more interesting, with sightseeing, accommodation and food options. As well as some lovely historic buildings, with a parador located in one of them, it is the epicentre of the famous Galician wine, Albariño. The town is packed with wine bars and restaurants celebrating the wine, and it's a great place to visit.

About 1km beyond the monastery, the Camino makes a short, steep descent from the road onto a track and follows it alongside a stream for 5km, past a series of watermills. The descent and tree roots make the track, otherwise really nice, a little challenging. To avoid this, follow the alternative route along the road.

After crossing beneath the motorway, the Camino continues off-road, including a lovely stretch along the riverbank all the way to Ponte Armelas, a small village with a coffee stop.

Ponte Armelas to Vilanova de Arousa **11km**

Follow the waymarks through a series of small villages down to the west-facing coastline, where the route joins a sandy track and heads north through campsites and over a bridge into Vilanova de Arousa.

THE TRASLATIO

The Traslatio refers to the route taken by the stone boat that carried the remains of St James to Santiago, and it is the only maritime stage of the Camino. It starts in Vilanova de Arousa and takes about 1hr 30min to reach Pontecesures, 1km from Padrón. Apparently, it's a lovely trip, visiting the mussel beds that supply the town's restaurants and the island of Cortegada, which is in the National Park of the Islands of Galicia and home to Europe's largest laurel forest. At least one ferry carries bikes, and the cost per person is 30 Euros.

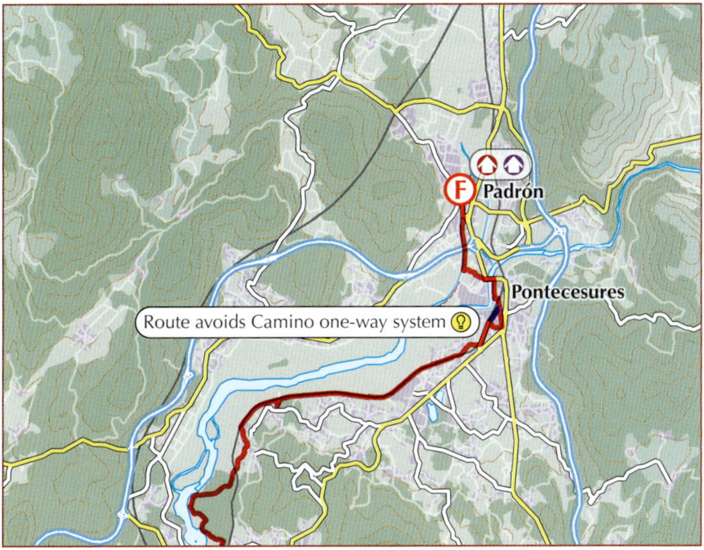

Vilanova de Arousa to Padrón 35km

The final part of the Spiritual Variant is flat and easy, and, with some minor variations, it is possible to follow the Camino all the way to Padrón. There is a stretch of seafront walkway between Vilagarcía and O Carril that is not open to cyclists, but the alternative route runs very close to the seafront. The approach to Padrón includes a 5km off-road stretch, primarily a sandy track through forest, with occasional views of the estuary.

From Padrón, continue to Santiago de Compostela (see Stage 4 of the Central Camino) for the final 26km of your Camino cycling adventure.

APPENDIX A

Accommodation

Lisbon to Porto on the Central Camino

Stage	Name	Location	Open	Sleeping rooms
1	Albergue Bom Caminha	Caminha	March to October	
2	A Casa Brava	Santarém	All year	Private rooms
2	Hotel Santarém	Santarém	All year	Private rooms
2	Hotel Vitoria	Santarém	All year	Private rooms
2	N1 Hostel Apartments & Suites	Santarém	All year	Different formats including dormitories
2	Villa Graça	Santarém	All year	Own room
2	Lezíria Park Hotel	Vila Franca de Xira	All year	Private rooms
3	Hotel dos Templários	São João Batista	All year	177
3	Pensão União	São João Batista		
3	Residencial Cavaleiros de Cristo	São João Batista		
3	Hotel Kamanga	Santa Maria dos Olivais	All year	
3	Vila Galé Collection Tomar	Santa Maria dos Olivais	All year	
3	Hotel República	Tomar	All year	19
3	Hotel Trovador	Tomar	All year	Private rooms
3	O Paço	Tomar	All year	
3	Thomar Boutique Hotel	Tomar		

Hotel
B&B/guesthouse

	Type	Tel	Web / email	Comments
	Hotel	+351963528441	bomcaminha.com	
	B&B/guesthouse	+351912852261		Bed & breakfast
	Hotel	+351243328191	santaremhotel.net	
	Hotel	+351243309130		Basic hotel
	Hotel	+351243350140	n1hostelapartments.com / info@n1hostelapartments.com	Various formats of accommodation available including single sex dormitories
	Hotel	+351243327127	villagraca.pt	Great location, nice rooms
	Hotel	+351263276670	leziriaparquehotel.pt	Not that bike friendly on one of my visits
	Hotel	+351249310100	hoteldostemplarios.com	
	Hotel	+351249323161	tomarhoteiscavcristoeuniao.com	
	Hotel			
	Hotel	+351249311555	hotelkamanga.com	
	Hotel	+351249249820	vilagale.com	
	Hotel	+351249193400	hotelrepublica.pt	
	Hotel	+351249322567	hoteltrovador.com-book.com	
	Hotel	+351910765737	pacotomar.pt	
	Hotel	+351249323210	thomarboutiquehotel.com	

Stage	Name	Location	Open	Sleeping rooms
4	Adega Típica	Ansião	All year	
4	Ansiturismo - Alojamento	Ansião	All year	Private rooms
5	Archisuites	Santa Clara	All year	Large rooms
5	Guest House Santa Clara	Coimbra		6 private rooms
5	Hotel Ibis	Alta	All year	110
5	Hotel Mondego	Baixa		
5	Hotel Oslo	Baixa	All year	Private rooms
6	Estalagem dos Padres	Albergaria-a-Velha		
6	Hotel Conde de Águeda	Águeda	All year	
7	Hotel Black Tulip	Mafamude		
7	Hotel Boa-Vista Porto	Foz do Douro	All year	
7	Hotel Vila Galé Ribeira Porto	Cedofeita	All year	
7	Hotel Vincci Ponte de Ferro	Centro Histórico	All year	
7	Hotel Vincci Porto	São Pedro da Afurada	24/7	95
7	Ribeira do Porto Hotel	Zona Histórica do Porto		

Type	Tel	Web / email	Comments
	+351236677364	reservas@adegatipodeansiao.com	
	+351236673337	ansiturismo.com / geral@ansiturismo.com	Modern and good value
	+351239440582	riversuites.pt	Has bike storage
	+351936961479	hoteisweb.com / guest-house-santa-clara/	Lovely hotel in a great location for the route
	+351239852130	ibis.com/gb/hotel-1672-ibis-coimbra-centro/index.shtml	Check for bike storage
	+351239496239	hotelmondego.com	Have bike storage but space is limited so check before confirming booking
	+351239829071	hoteloslo-coimbra.pt	Close to route
	+351930610380	upliving.pt/en	
	+351234610390	hotelcondedagueda.com	
	+351223748020	hotelblacktulip.pt	
	+351225320020	hotelboavista.com	Nice hotel, charge for bike storage
	+351223748020	reservas.vilagale.com/engine/search	Have parking so should be OK for bikes
	0351220902900	en.vinccipontedeferro.com	
	+351220439620	vincciporto.com	Has bike storage
	+351222032097	ribeiradoportohotel.com	No private garage so question mark on bike storage

Porto to Santiago de Compostela on the Central Camino

Stage	Name	Location	Open	Sleeping rooms
1	Hotel Dom Nuno	Barcelos	All Year	
1	Hotel Restaurante Bagoeira	Hotel Restaurante Bagoeira	All year	
1	Top'Otel	Barcelinhos	All year	
1	Villa C Hotel & SPA	Azurara	All year	43
2	Albergue de Peregrinos de Tui	Tui		36 bunks
2	A torre do xudeu	Tui	All year	6
2	Hostal Albergue La Sigrina	Tui	All year	
2	Parador de Tui	Tui		32
2	Alojamento da Vila	Valença		
2	Lara	Valença		
2	Pousada de Sao Teotónio	Valença	All year	
2	Império do Norte	Ponte de Lima	All year	
2	InLima Hotel & Spa	Ponte de Lima	All year	
3	Hotel Galicia Palace	Pontevedra	All year	85
3	Hotel Virgen del Camino	Pontevedra	All year	
3	Parador Pontevedra	Pontevedra	All year	47
4	Hotel Rosalia	Padrón	All year	
4	Parador Hostal dos Reis Católicos	Santiago de Compostela	All year	137

Type	Tel	Web / email	Comments
	+351253812810	hoteldnunobarcelos.com	
	+351253809500	bagoeira.com	Good location, good value – check for bike storage
	+351253825090	topotel.pt	
		villacboutiquehotel.com	
	+34638276855		
	+34986603535	atorredoxudeo.es	
	+34654396782	lasigrinahostal.es	
	+34986600300	parador.es/es/paradores/parador-de-tui	Great accommodation if a little old fashioned
	+351251824348	hotellara.com	
	+351251800260	pousadas.pt/uk/hotel/pousada-de-valenca	
	+351253254197	hotelimperiodonorte.com	
	+351258900050	inlimahotel.com	Check for bike storage
	+34986864411	galiciapalace.com	
	+34986855900	booking.com	
	+34986855800	parador.es/es/paradores/parador-de-pontevedra	Bike storage available
	+34981812490	hotelrosalia.es	
	+34981582200	paradores.es/en/parador-de-santiago-de-compostela	

Porto to Santiago de Compostela on the Coastal Camino

Stage	Name	Location	Open	Sleeping rooms
1	Villa C Hotel & SPA	Azurara	All year	43
2	A Rendilheira	Vila do Conde	All year	
2	A Rendilheira Boutique Hotel	Vila do Conde		
2	Hotel Brazão	Vila do Conde	All year	30
2	Grande Hotel da Póvoa	Póvoa de Varzim	All year	
2	Hotel Costa Verde	Póvoa de Varzim	All year	
2	Hotel Jardim Viana	Viana do Castelo	All year	
2	Pousada Viana Do Castelo	Viana do Castelo	All year	
3	Albergue Bom Caminha	Caminha	March to October	
3	Eli-Mar	A Guarda	All year	
3	Hotel Convento de San Benito	A Guarda	All year	30
3	Hotel Vila Da Guarda	A Guarda	All year	26
3	Minho Belo	Lovelhe		
5	AC Hotel	Vigo	All year	
5	Hotel Ciudad de Vigo	Vigo	All year	
5	Hotel Anunciada	Baiona	All year	28
5	Parador Nacional de Baiona	Baiona	All year	

	Type	Tel	Web / email	Comments
		+351252240420	villaboutiquehotel.com	
		+351252615113		Great location
		+351252642016	hotelbrazao.pt	
		+351252290400	grandehoteldapovoa.com	
		+351252298600	hotelcostaverde.pt	
		+351258828915	hoteljardimviana.pt	
		+351258800370	pousadas.pt/en/hotel/pousada	Claims to have the best views in Portugal
		+351963528441	bomcaminha.com	
		+34986613000	eli-marhotel.com	
		+34986611166	hotelsanbenito.es	Bit out of the way
		+34986611121	hotelviladaguarda.com	
		+34986449250	marriott.com/en-us/hotels/vgopa-ac-hotel-palacio-universal/overview/	
		+34986227820	aldahotels.es/hoteles/galicia/pontevedra/vigo/hotel-alda-puerta-del-sol	
		+34986356018	hotel-anunciada.com	
		+34986355000	parador.es/es/paradores/parador-de-baiona	

Stage	Name	Location	Open	Sleeping rooms
5	Hotel Faro Silleiro	Percebelleira	All year	
5	NH Collection Hotels	Santiago de Vigo	All year	108

Spiritual Variant

Stage	Name	Location	Open	Sleeping rooms
1	Caroi Hostel	A Escusa		
1	Mosteiro de Santa Maria da Armenteira	A Escusa	All year	
1	Pousada de Armenteira	A Escusa	All year	
1	Hospedería Monasterio de Poio	O Convento		
1	Hotel Arco Iris	Vilanova de Arousa	All Year	
1	Hotel Bradomín	Vilanova de Arousa		
1	Hotel Dinajan	Vilanova de Arousa		52
1	Parador de Cambados	Cambados	All year	
1	Real Cambados	Cambados	All year	

Type	Tel	Web / email	Comments
	+34986499483	farosilleirohotel.com	Boutique hotel with an infinity pool and great views
	+34986433643	nh-hoteles.es/hoteles/vigo	

Type	Tel	Web / email	Comments
		monasteriodearmenteira.es	Imposing Romanesque/ Gothic monastery set in lovely grounds. Nice place for a break
	+34986716372	eurostarshotels.com/pousada-de-armenteira.html	
	+34986770000	monasteriodepoio.es	
	+34986555444	arcoirisweb.net/index.html	
		hotel-bradomin.com	
	+34986561534	hoteldinajan.es	
	+34986542250	parador.es	
	+34986524404	hotelrealcambados.com	

APPENDIX B

Useful information

Credentials and advice

Lisbon Pilgrim Office
Igreja da Conceição Velha, Rua da Alfândega, Lisbon
Open afternoons for credentials and advice.

Pilgrims' Hostel do Porto
Rua Barão de Forrester, 954, Porto
Open year-round, 2-10pm
tel +351 220 140 515

Bike hire and other services

Bikeiberia
Perfect location for collecting a bike in Lisbon, but will deliver and collect the bike in Santiago de Compostela.
bikeiberia.com
info@bikeiberia.com
tel +351 969630369

Cycle Rentals
Good value and a big choice of bikes. Will deliver and collect bikes.
cycling-rentals.com

Go-Cycling
Offices in Lisbon and Porto
gocyclingportugal.com
info@gocyclingportugal.com
tel +351969154589

Turisbike
Offer a bespoke tour planning service including bike hire, accommodation booking and luggage transfer, located near Vila do Conde.
tours@turisbike.com
tel +351 252 219 000

Bicigrino
One of the longest-established bike rental and luggage transfer providers.
caminosantiagobike@gmail.com
tel +34 972 90 87 27

Several companies offer to pick up your bike and send it to an address in Portugal. Beware, your bike can get stuck in customs.

Coach transfers

Coaches are a great way of traveling with a packed bike in Portugal and Spain. The most comprehensive networks are provided by:
Alsa
alsa.com

Rede Expressos
rede-expressos.pt

For the growing number of cyclists who prefer not to fly, consider taking a coach all the way with a packed bike in luggage. It's a 38-hour journey from London to Lisbon.

Flixbus
flixbus.co.uk

Train travel

For the latest on how to take your bike across Europe on a train, go to:
The Man in Seat Sixty-One
seat61.com

Festivals

Month	Day	Festival	Location
Portugal			
February/March		International Film Festival	Porto
March/April		Easter	National
April	25	Liberty Day	National
May	1	Labour Day	National
May	Early	Festival of the Crosses	Barcelos
	Mid	Burning of the Ribbons	Coimbra
	Late	May Fair	Azambuja
May/June		Corpus Christi	National
June	Early	National Agricultural Fair	Santarém
	10	Portuguese National Day	National
	12,13	St Anthony's Day	Lisbon
	23,24	St John's Day	Porto, Vila do Condo
	Late	Horse Fair	Ponte de Lima
July	Early	Red Waistcoat Festival	Vila Franca de Xira
	Whole month	Águeda Art Festival	Águeda
	Early	International Short Film Festival	Vila do Conde
	4	Saint Isabel Festival	Coimbra
August	15	Festival of the Assumption	National
	Mid	Pilgrimage of Our Lady of Agony	Viano do Castelo
September	Mid	New Fair	Ponte de Lima
October	5	Republic Day	National
	Mid	Can Festival	Coimbra
	Late	National Gastronomy Festival	Santarém
November	1	All Saints Day	National
	First Half	National Horse Fair	Golegã
December	1	Independence Day	National
Spain			
March	End	Reconquest of Vigo	Vigo
April	Mid	Festival of San Telmo	Tui
May	1	Labour Day	National

Month	Day	Festival	Location
	Mid	Cuttlefish Festival	Redondela
	6	St John of Lightening Festival	Padrón
	25	Ascension Festival	Santiago
June	24	St John's Day	Caldas de Reis
July	11	St Benedict's Day	Pontevedra
	18	St Marina's Day	Baiona
	25	St James Day	Santiago
August	15	Assumption	National
	16	San Roque Festival	Santiago,Vigo, Caldas de Reis
	Mid	Festival of the Virgin Pilgrim	Pontevedra
September	25	Santisimo Cristo de la Agonia Festival	O Porriño
	26	San Cosmer and San Damian Festival	Biano
October	12	National Day	National
November	1	All Saints Day	National
December	6	Spanish Constitution Day	National
	8	Feast of the Immaculate Conception	National

CICERONE

Hello, and thank you for choosing a Cicerone guide!

It takes the combined dedication of many to create the book you now hold. Our authors explore the world to find the best routes; they research, write, record data and take stunning photos on the trail to inspire and guide new adventures. Then, our talented team work together with authors to create the best products for our readers, whether digital or printed. The final part of the picture is you; we deeply value hearing from Cicerone customers with ideas and updates from the trail. Your input helps us to improve and innovate across our guides.

Cicerone is proud to be a family business. Exploring the outdoors has always been central to our lives, and we are passionate about sharing our love of walking, trekking, cycling and climbing. If you have any feedback or just want to say hello, please get in touch – we would love to hear from you.

Happy adventuring,
Joe & Maddy

Joe Maddy

Contact us at

hello@cicerone.co.uk **cicerone.co.uk/contact**

The Cicerone range

- International walking & trekking
- British walking & long distance
- Pilgrimages
- Short walks
- Via ferrata, climbing & scrambling
- Cycling, mountain biking & bikepacking
- Winter climbs & snow sports
- Trail & fell running

Discover more at **cicerone.co.uk/activities**

Our formats

App

A digitised version of the guidebook's expert-curated routes, with interactive maps, detailed facilities information and offline GPS navigation

Guidebook

The complete guidebook with detailed descriptions, route and facilities information, profiles and maps in an easy-to-use printed format

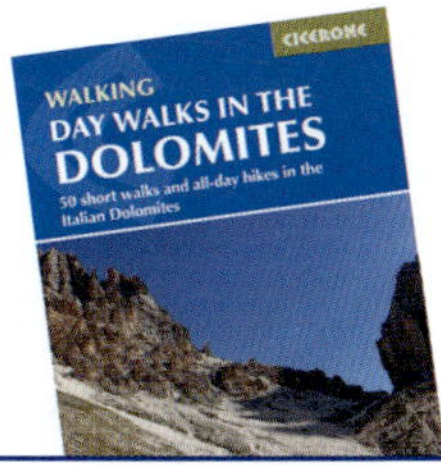

eBook

The digital edition of the guidebook with detailed descriptions, route and facilities information, profiles and maps, ready to use on any device

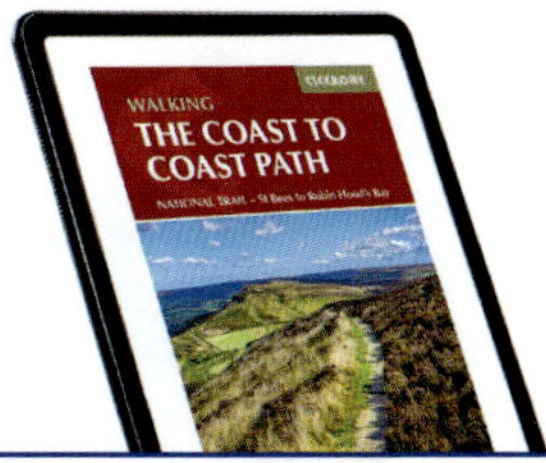

GPX files

Download GPX route files from your account to use on compatible devices for easy navigation and planning

See available formats for this book at **cicerone.co.uk/1304**

GPX files

Download free GPX files for this book

cicerone.co.uk/1304/GPX

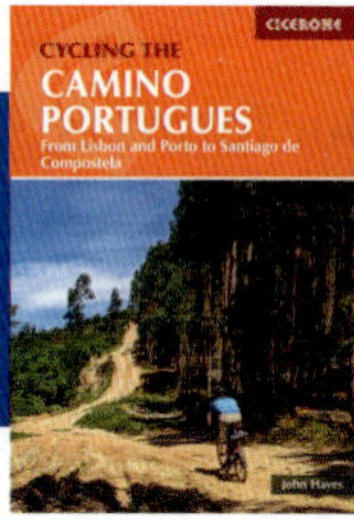

Other cycling touring guides

Other guides to this region

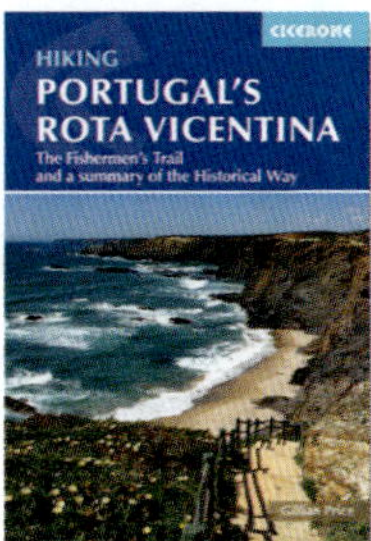

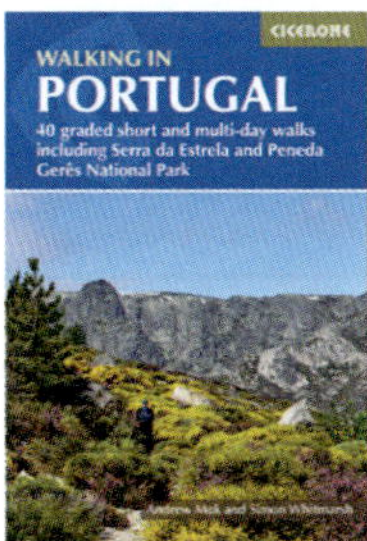

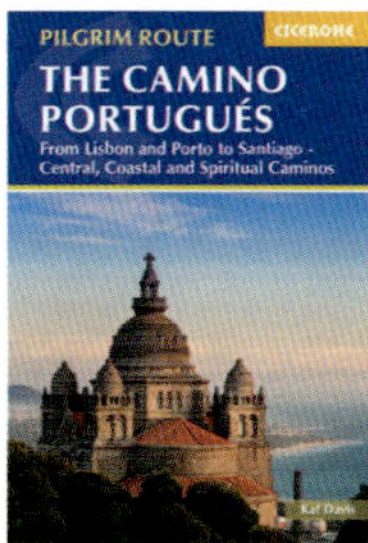

Trust Cicerone to guide your next adventure

cicerone.co.uk